Kim Atman

Forbidden Questions About Abortion

More to Life Publishing

Forbidden Questions About Abortion

By:

Kim Atman

Published by:

More to Life Publishing

P. O. Box 92, Emigrant,
MT 59027, U. S. A.
Phone: (406) 333-4513

Copyright © 1993.
First printing 1993.
Printed in the United States of America

Library of Congress Cataloging in Publication Data
Catalog Card Number: 92-062637
Kim Atman
Forbidden Questions About Abortion
1. Abortion

ISBN 0-9632564-6-7: $ 12.95 Softcover.

Table of Contents

X

Table of Contents

Table of Contents

Table of Contents

FOREWORD

Dear reader . . .

Have you ever considered that the abortion debate could be used as a mirror to show us something about ourselves and our society? Let me explain what I mean.

At the time I am writing this, two abortion doctors have been shot and several abortion clinics have been burned to the ground. Numerous pro-life activists have been arrested and there have been hundreds of violent clashes between pro-life and pro-choice proponents. In my opinion, the really shocking part of all this violence is that it is done *by* people *to* people.

What does this show us about ourselves? It shows us that the abortion debate has caused a great number of us to look upon other people as enemies. It seems as if many of the players on both sides of the abortion debate automatically see anyone with a different opinion about abortion as the enemy. However, doctors performing abortions are still human beings as are pro-lifers blocking entry to an abortion clinic.

I see this as a cause for great concern because history has shown us what can happen when people begin to look at each other as enemies. Tensions grow, leading to outbreaks of violence that get progressively worse until we have a war-like scenario in which people are seeking to destroy each other.

Take note of what is really happening in this process. It begins with two factions who both believe they are fighting for a just cause. However, at some point a transition occurs, and from then on the cause is no longer the driving force. Instead of fighting to champion a cause, people are fighting to destroy the enemy. The original cause has simply become an excuse for wholesale destruction of other people. Both factions have now forgotten, or are willfully ignoring, that their opponents are human beings just like themselves. Instead people treat each other like objects that can be justly destroyed for the cause.

I believe most of us can point to examples of this type of conflict from history, such as religious wars and ethnic conflicts. When we look back at these events decades later, it can be very difficult to understand how they happened. No longer caught up in the emotional energies of the situation, we realize a very simple fact of life: No cause can ever justify the destruction of other people!

In my opinion society must make a choice. We can choose to let the abortion debate continue on the track it has been following for two decades or we can seek to change the focus of the debate.

If we allow the abortion debate to continue unchanged, one does not have to be a prophet to predict the outcome. We will see more and more violence and whatever the actual scenario may be, it will be ugly. If we do not want to sit back and watch our country slide into a situation that resembles a civil war, our only option is to change something in the debate.

The basic question behind this book is: What can we do to shift the abortion debate in a more constructive direction? My theory is that our very first step must be to consider how the debate has been influenced by our paradigms.

The term paradigm has been used in a number of self-motivation books. One of the best explanations of this idea is given in the book *The 7 Habits of Highly Effective People* by Stephen R. Covey. The word paradigm comes from Greek and means a platform or frame of reference from which we look at the world. Stephen Covey illustrates this with the difference between a map and the actual location. If we are going to a specific location in downtown Chicago but are equipped with a map over Detroit, we will obviously have great difficulty getting where we want to go. The map symbolizes our frame of reference, our paradigm, and it is obvious that unless we change our paradigm, we will be lost forever. A pair of yellow glasses is another symbol of a paradigm. The world is obviously not yellow, but as long as we are wearing the glasses we will see it as such. If we wore the glasses long enough we might begin to believe they give an accurate picture of reality. If we were born with the glasses, we might never question our picture of a yellow world.

An Open Mind
Is the Basis for Progress

One of the first people to describe the importance of paradigms was Thomas Kuhn who showed that almost every break-through in any field of science happened because scientists questioned the old beliefs, the established way of thinking—the paradigms. We could say that the basis for all progress is a willingness to look beyond our paradigms, to ask new questions. It then follows that when there is a lack of progress the cause could be that we have not been willing to question our existing beliefs. In other words, the basis for progress in any human endeavor is open-mindedness. Does the lack of a peaceful resolution in the abortion debate show that we have become entrapped by certain paradigms?

When it comes to open-mindedness, we can talk about three different approaches. Some people are completely open and will adopt any new idea that comes their way. They often end up being quite confused, with little personal integrity. Other people have completely closed their minds and refuse to question their chosen beliefs. They often end up with a very narrow-minded attitude towards life and can become outright fanatical.

However, most of us are somewhere in between these two extremes; we have what we might call "selective open-mindedness." There are some issues on which we are quite open-minded, but there are some beliefs, certain psychologically foundational principals, that we are very reluctant to question. The reason for this is that it can be a very emotional experience to question our existing belief system. Letting go of an old belief can cause us great pain and we sometimes see it as a threat to our personal integrity. However, history shows us that personal growth as well as growth in society often makes it necessary for us to go through the emotional pain of letting go of our old beliefs.

I have noticed that most of us have a tendency to close our minds concerning certain issues. We are definitely not fanatics in general, but it seems like certain stimuli can trigger us into closing our minds. Most of the time we have our normal open-minded attitude, but certain subjects can push us into a very rigid frame of mind that often causes us to say or do things that are out of character. I think most of us know people, who are very easygoing towards everyone except one particular person. The mere mention of a name can cause their outer appearance to change to the point where they seem to be an entirely different person. Other people react in a similar way when it comes to one particular issue and just one wrong word can have the same effect as waving a red flag in front of a bull. I think some people react this way towards the abortion issue and that this reaction is one of the major obstacles to changing the course of the debate. When people have a closed mind they will automatically see any attempt to make them reconsider their position as a personal threat.

What I hope all of my readers will understand and remember is that this book is not meant to be the final word on abortion. It is not an attack on you personally or on your present beliefs. I do not see persons who disagree with me as enemies. It is not my intention with this book to change the opinions of people who are already firmly pro-life or pro-choice. But recent polls have shown that most Americans actually reject both extremes in the abortion debate. I believe this shows us that most people are not firmly anchored in either of the two camps, which must mean that they are open to a new way of looking at the issue. This book is written specifically for people with an open-minded attitude and it is an attempt to provide a more diversified perspective than is currently available. One of the persons who saw a preview copy of this book got so angry that he refused to read it all. He was not able to see the book as simply an attempt to question our paradigms, but felt personally threatened by it.

Let me hasten to point out that since I am not a full-time scholar, I simply do not have the time to research everything in detail. Trying to fully support every idea I am presenting would add another hundred pages to the book which would make it so long that many people would refuse to read it. So, for more detailed information, I refer the reader to the books mentioned throughout.

Finally, I am not trying to present something that is an

absolute proof, but a catalogue of ideas. I am merely trying to point in a new direction and present a number of the questions I believe we need to ask. I hope other people, whether they agree with my ideas or not, will take up the torch and breathe new life into the abortion debate. The basic idea I want to get across is that we need to look for a broader perspective on the issue of abortion. If you end up agreeing with that and nothing else, then I will consider the book a success.

If the reader approaches the book expecting to be provoked, then this expectation will probably be confirmed. It is a common reaction that people will pick out one idea that they do not agree with and use it as an excuse for rejecting a book, a person or a philosophical system. But, just as beauty is in the eyes of the beholder, I think the value of this book will depend on the reader's willingness to consider the ideas as suggestions instead of threats.

If you have a greater knowledge of the subjects covered in the book, or if you think there are other issues that should have been included, please write your thoughts down and send them to me. I am very open to doing another book in which a number of people, whether they agree with me or not, present new and different perspectives on the abortion issue.

What Is a Forbidden Question?

Let me conclude by explaining the expression "forbidden questions." In the so-called Dark Ages the rulers of medieval Europe persecuted people for saying that the earth was not flat. The ruling powers defined the question "Is the earth really flat?" as a "forbidden question." However, the kings and the churches of medieval Europe did not do this out of evil intent. They really believed that the earth was flat, it was one of their most basic paradigms. Since they had absolute power, they sought to force their paradigm upon society.

What we must realize is that even in a free, democratic society we have paradigms. They may not be put upon us through physical force, but they can be programmed into our minds because we were brought up to accept them without question. Our paradigms will inevitably create a number of "forbidden questions." It may be questions that we are unable to formulate because we are too entrapped by our paradigms. Or, it may be questions we refuse to ask because doing so would mean too much emotional pain. My hope is that this book will make some of my readers realize that asking the "forbidden questions" can open up new possibilities for a peaceful resolution to the abortion debate and for personal growth as well.

Abortion is such an emotional issue that the thought of writing a book about it can be almost paralyzing. No matter what one might write about abortion, some people will be violently opposed to it. My greatest concern is that some readers will approach the book with only one question is mind: "Is he pro-life or pro-choice?" As soon as they find something that points either way, they will put me in a nice little box and from then on their minds will be closed. They will either refuse to read the rest of the book or they will read it only to refute everything in it that does not agree with their paradigms. So, in order to get off to a soft start I would like to begin by touching upon a subject that most of us should be able to agree upon: The value of democracy.

PART ONE

The Foundation

Democracy and the Human Psyche

CHAPTER 1

Has the Abortion Debate Subverted the Democratic Process?

The democratic process is supposed to enable us to resolve conflicts without violence. So, here is the first forbidden question we need to ask: Why hasn't the democratic process worked in the abortion debate?

To answer this question I think we should begin by considering why we created democracies in the first place. Democracy, being only a little over 200 years old, is a new phenomenon on this planet. For the better part of known history, humankind has lived in societies with some form of highly centralized power structure. In a non-democratic society the issue of abortion would have been much easier to handle since all decisions are made by the elite in power. Such a power elite would have decided either for or against abortion and that would have been the end of it. The advantage of this system is that the process of making and implementing decisions is much simpler. A totalitarian nation can respond faster and more decisively to an internal crisis or to the threat of an outer enemy.

In contrast, a democracy will often be paralyzed by disagreement and decades can be spent debating back and forth. So why did we abandon these seemingly more efficient societies to create a more cumbersome democratic form of government? The basic reason is that the simpler decision-making of a totalitarian system is also its major disadvantage. In the vast majority of totalitarian societies we see the same pattern occur.

Since the members of the ruling elite are not elected, they do not have much personal accountability. This causes them to become gradually more abusive towards the people and as a result we have a division of society into two distinct groups. There is a small elite with a monopoly on power, wealth and other privileges and, then, a subdued majority with very limited opportunities for improving their lives. If the king or emperor is unintelligent, power-hungry, insane, or outright malicious, then the suffering of the people can be tremendous. A typical example of such a society is Medieval Europe in which the king had absolute power, the noble class owned all land and the merchants had a monopoly on trade.

I think most of us can agree that a totalitarian society can be characterized by one word: Injustice. When a small elite can dominate a majority of the population by holding special privileges, then we have an unjust society.

This demonstrates that the origin and continued survival of democratic societies depends on a mechanism in the human psyche—our ability to recognize injustice.

The Psychological Basis for Democracy

Our next step must be to consider what it is that allows us to recognize injustice.

Today most of us can see that the feudal societies were based on injustice, but the kings and noblemen of the time would not have agreed with us. They believed they had an absolute right to hold special privileges and they did not see it as injustice. The reason is that a totalitarian society is functioning according to the law of the jungle and therefore, might is right. If you have property that I want, and if I am stronger than you are, then I have the right to take your property. If you resist me, I have a right to eliminate you if I can.

What this means is that a person can act out his or her immediate desires without considering how it will affect others in the long term. In such a society the most self-centered people will automatically have the upper hand since they have the drive to assert themselves above others. People who are honest and self-sacrificing will be no match for the aggressive egomaniacs who are willing to do anything to gain personal power. That is why a power elite in a totalitarian society often becomes so abusive—it attracts a certain type of people. These people are living as if the ends could justify the means, they believe the fulfillment of their personal desires is more important than anything else.

The egomaniacs do not see any injustice in a feudal society, so why do we say there is injustice? Because somewhere inside us we know with absolute certainty that it is not right for a person to do whatever he wants if it causes harm to others. A society allowing some people to fulfill their immediate desires by taking freedom from other people is an unjust society.

The ability to recognize injustice is based on the realization that there is something more important than the fulfillment of our immediate desires. It is the idea that every human being has a set of basic rights that cannot be violated by anyone even if they are stronger or more aggressive. A democratic society is based on the idea that certain timeless principles are more important than the temporary desires of any one person. Without principles there would be no way to define injustice since different people would come up with their own, personal opinions.

One of the unfortunate effects of being born in a democratic society is that we tend to take our freedom for granted—but think about it for a minute. For most of history, humankind lived as if nothing was more important than the fulfillment of the immediate desires of a small elite. Then, only 200 years ago, we decided that this is not right and that all our personal desires should be compared to an impersonal standard. This "standard" is not even a material object, it is just an idea; a set of principles that seemingly appeared out of nowhere. A medieval king would say that it is a product of our imagination and that he can see no reason why our personal beliefs should be more important than his. However, we say that inalienable rights are not the product of our minds, we did not invent them, we merely recognized them. They did not originate in the human mind, but on a higher level of existence which means that no human being has the authority to override them.

This is a complete break with historical tradition and, when you think about it, it is simply earth-shattering. Instead of the belief that some people belong to an elite with special rights, we now say that all human beings have equal rights.

There is also a more practical aspect of the recognition of

rights, since a totalitarian society does not offer much protection to anyone. By creating a society in which certain timeless principles are more important than the desires of the moment, we gain protection from what we may call the lower aspects of human nature. The creation of democratic nations shows that humankind as a whole has matured into a new realization of what is enlightened self-interest.

According to this, it may seem as if the fundamental difference between a democracy and a totalitarian system is the recognition of principles. I disagree; the recognition of principles will do nothing in itself. The real difference between democracy and totalitarianism is the *respect* for principles. A totalitarian dictator may actually recognize that his subjects have certain rights. But these rights will be defined by the state and the leader can at any given moment suspend or change the rights if it fits his agenda. A totalitarian nation may also give special rights to a part of the population, thereby institutionalizing the existence of a privileged elite.

In its purest form, a democracy is based on a set of human rights that are *not* defined by the state. At no time can the leaders of society choose to suspend or change these basic rights and they may not give special privileges to certain people. Unfortunately, we human beings sometimes seem to forget about the importance of principles.

In the foreword I mentioned the book by Stephen R. Covey and the description of paradigms. According to Covey, there are two opposing tendencies working in our psychology—he says that we can be either self-centered or principle-centered. It is his opinion that our society over the past 50 years has become more self-centered by embracing what he calls the personality ethic. He believes that the key to personal success and happiness is to transcend this self-centeredness and get back to a set of principles that are bigger than ourselves.

(At this point I hear some of my readers saying: "Aha, I see what he is getting at! A few pages down the road he is going to turn around and say that everyone with a certain attitude towards abortion is ego-centered." But I don't think life is that simple, so don't throw the book against the wall just yet.)

A Pseudo Debate

Since the respect for principles is the very basis for a democracy, let's consider what happens to a democratic debate if this respect begins to fade.

According to British historian Arnold Toynbee, any society, be it totalitarian or democratic, can only survive for a long period of time if it provides a tool for a peaceful resolution of human conflict. Otherwise it will be divided and it will either be taken over by an outer enemy or it will disintegrate from within—or both. In a democracy the tool for resolving conflict is a public debate in which everyone is free to express his or her opinion. Let us take note of the basic principle involved. Human interaction is full of conflicting viewpoints, and a debate will often begin with two sides holding apparently opposite, incompatible positions. The goal of a free, democratic debate is to search for a higher understanding of the issue. This should make both sides realize that their original positions were based on a limited perspective and therefore not the highest understanding possible. As a result, people will realize that what seemed to be an unsolvable conflict was simply the product of a limited understanding of certain aspects of life. By bringing forth a higher understanding, we eliminate the conflict and people are able to see beyond their original positions. This unrestricted debate should ideally lead to a situation in which the vast majority of the population takes a clear and united stand based on a new and higher understanding of the issue. Because of this unity, their decision deserves implementation through the laws of society. If there is a minority who cannot accept the new position, they should accept the ruling of the majority as the necessary price we all have to pay to uphold a democratic nation. In this way an issue is resolved and conflict is replaced by harmony.

The only problem is that a democratic debate cannot, in itself, guarantee a resolution. When we have two parties with opposing views, a true resolution can only happen if the debaters are willing to look for a higher understanding. If all the people involved cling to the opinion they had at the beginning of the debate and refuse to reconsider the issue in an unbiased way, how can there be resolution? It is essential that we realize the importance of principles, since they offer us the only way to find a higher understanding. If we begin to ignore principles, a debate becomes a battle between man-made paradigms, and it can literally go on forever.

When a democratic debate is dragging on and leading to violence, there is only one possible explanation. The participants in the debate have forgotten the importance of higher principles—they have become self-centered. They want to hold onto their original opinions and they are no longer willing to compare their personal beliefs to a set of timeless principles.

If a democratic debate does not revolve around the same principles that a democracy is based on, then it can never be resolved peacefully. It may lead to a situation in which one group of people has managed to assert its opinion over another group by having its self-centered ideas implemented through the laws of society. This does not resolve the conflict because the losing faction will not abandon their previous position. Instead, they will seek to fight what they see as an unjust suppression of their, equally self-centered, ideas and they may even seek revenge. This creates a downward spiral resulting in the violent conflict that the democratic process was meant to avoid.

In the foreword I described a mechanism whereby certain stimuli can trigger us into closing our minds and refusing to look beyond our paradigms. We can now see that what happens in this process is that we become triggered into ignoring principles and allowing our minds to become self-centered.

How can we determine when a society has become self-centered? It is quite simple. Whenever people begin to treat each other as things, when they act as if the ends could justify the means, as if a cause (even a just cause) can justify the destruction of people, then we have a case of self-centeredness. If everyone was principle-centered, a difference of opinion would never lead to violence because it would not cause people to see their opponents as enemies.

By focusing on principles we are able to see beyond our personal egos and we do not feel threatened by people with a different opinion. Instead of seeking to assert our own position, as a form of emotional self-defense, we can avoid being caught up in a maelstrom of emotions. By focusing on principles we can find a new and higher position on the issue that goes beyond the opinions we started out with. In a principle-centered debate both sides will win because they become liberated from paradigms that limited their personal growth.

If the leaders, or even a large part of the people, in a

democratic nation have become self-centered and no longer respect timeless principles, then the democratic process cannot work. Most of us were brought up to believe in the paradigm that there is a fundamental difference between democracy and totalitarianism. We can now see that this is not so—the only difference is whether the leadership is self-centered or principle-centered.

This realization tells us that we must revise another of our paradigms, namely the idea that a democracy in itself will guarantee freedom and justice. The only factor that can secure freedom and justice is a process in the human psyche. Respect is a feeling and feelings do not take place on a piece of paper, in certain official buildings or, for that matter, on television. Feelings take place in the psyche of the individual. On the basis of this observation I would like to propose a new concept for solving problems in a democratic nation.

Most of the phenomenon taking place in our society can be traced back to certain processes in the human psyche. If we do not understand the psychological mechanism involved, we cannot hope to understand what is happening in society. If we do not seek to solve our problems by incorporating this understanding of the human psyche, it will be very difficult to cope with many of the problems we see in society.

Principle Versus Ego

Because of these observations we can see that both a totalitarian and a democratic system are based on two different tendencies in the human psyche.

When I read the classical literature on philosophy and religion, as well as modern writings on psychology and self-improvement, it is very clear to me that there are two opposing forces working in our psychology. Most human actions spring from a desire, without desires we would essentially be robots. The problem is that both our desires and the ways we seek to fulfill them can be self-centered or principle-centered. Our ability and willingness to evaluate desires and their resulting actions according to this standard is the difference between a primitive and a civilized human being.

When we are self-centered, we use whatever power is available to us, or whatever we think we can get away with, to fulfill our immediate desires. We do not consider how this will affect others or how it will affect ourselves in the long run. Being self-centered takes away our ability to consider long-term perspectives. The tendency for self-centeredness is what leads to a totalitarian society in which the egomaniacs dominate the more normal people.

When we are principle-centered, we realize two basic facts of life:

1. We have both immediate and long-term desires and to find happiness we must balance the two. If we only consider our immediate desires, we may destroy the possibility for fulfilling long-term desires.

2. We live in a world of cause and effect, as described by Newton's law of action and reaction. Everything we do has an effect that reaches beyond ourselves. It produces consequences; consequences which will often return to affect us. So, unless we consider the possible consequences, we cannot know if the price we have to pay is worth the benefit gained by fulfilling an immediate desire.

It is this ability to see principles as enlightened self-interest that gives rise to a democratic society.

According to this discourse, timeless principles are meant to serve us as guidelines that will allow us to avoid being dominated by the lower aspects of human nature. If that is so, then here is the central question of human existence: Why aren't we always principle-centered? Why are we doing things that harm ourselves? The obvious answer is that we don't always see what is best for us because something in our own psyche is preventing our clear vision.

This is the basic dichotomy in human existence and from the earliest recorded history until today philosophers have sought to understand the two forces. We could call these tendencies the ego and the super-ego, the lower self and the higher self or whatever we want. I don't think the name is very important, the main thing is that we recognize that our psyche is a battlefield between two opposing forces.

It is my personal opinion that the realization of this basic mechanism in the human psyche is the missing link in the evolution of democracies. It is the key that will allow our democratic nations to live up to their fullest potential. How can we expect democracy to work if we have not made an all-out effort to understand the basic psychological mechanism involved? We have now been engaged in the democratic experiment for 200 years, yet we do not understand the most basic force driving this experiment. We don't understand what allows us to recognize principles and what causes us to ignore them. If we had not developed an understanding of the force of gravity, we would never have been able to overcome this force and send man to the moon. Right now, democracy is like a big, mindless machine plunging forward heedlessly because we have not yet found out how to direct its course. We haven't yet decided to grab the steering wheel located in our own psyche!

I think these observations provide an important key to understanding the present abortion debate. By considering the self-centered tendency in human psychology it becomes far easier to understand why democracy sometimes cannot produce results and why our society seems to be in a gridlock. I believe most of us have been programmed to believe in the paradigm that democracy automatically guarantees principle-centered leadership. We tend to believe that if someone has attained a position of power in the government or in a large organization (such as the pro-life or pro-choice movements) he or she must be principle-centered. I think we should abandon this paradigm and realize that the only difference between freedom and some form of tyranny is the choice each of us must make between higher principles and the human ego.

CHAPTER 2

Has the Human Ego Subverted the Abortion Debate?

Now that we have pointed to a mechanism in the human psyche as part of the problem, I think we should try to identify this mechanism. I want to make it clear that I am not trying to give a complete psychological discourse on this point, only a brief, and therefore somewhat simplistic, summary.

The two best known faculties in our psyche are the emotions and the intellect, but neither of them allows us to recognize timeless principles.

The human intellect is a wonderful tool for analyzing and evaluating situations and ideas. However, many people are beginning to realize that there is a limit to what the intellect can do for us because it is functioning on a certain level of reality; one could say in a special world. This world is a relative world, a world where everything is defined by its relationship to something else. The intellect thinks in terms of polarities. Consequently, it is very easy to set up an intellectual philosophy describing the world as a product of relative opposites. Everything is put on a scale and is defined according to its position on this scale. Light is on one side of a scale, darkness on the other side; good and evil are opposites on another scale and so on. The intellect cannot handle the idea that there could be something that cannot be put on a relative scale, such as timeless principles. To the intellect, such principles are simply a product of our minds and we can choose to accept them or not. We can also reason for or against them, and thus, when we consider absolute values with the intellect, they automatically become relative, because that is the only way the intellect can deal with them. Since the intellect can only deal with an idea in a comparative or relative sense, we cannot use it to resolve moral or ethical questions. The intellect cannot solve these problems because it cannot transcend its own relativity.

Our emotions also function in their own relative, ever changing world, unable to discriminate between relative values and timeless principles. Emotions can give us a strong, creative drive and the enthusiasm that is capable of producing the greatest of human achievements. Emotions are also responsible for creating some of the worst human tragedies. Therefore, if we allow our emotions to direct the course of our society we will most likely be on a roller coaster of ups and downs.

What we see is that it is neither the intellect, nor the emotions that allow us to identify injustice because they cannot deal with absolute principles, only with relative values. An inalienable right is an absolute statement, a statement that we cannot argue for or against. "Thou shalt not kill" is such a statement. The first reaction of the human intellect to an absolute statement is: "Why not?" The next reaction is to define conditions under which it is acceptable or not acceptable to kill, and then the absolute has become relative. Our emotions can easily cause us to slip into a state of consciousness in which killing becomes not only acceptable but desirable. Consequently, we see that the idea behind a free democracy is based on neither our intellect nor our emotions because these two faculties do not allow us to discriminate between right and wrong in an absolute sense.

Inalienable rights are based on something that forms a golden middle way between intellect and emotions. It is an ability to go within, to contact something not affected by outer conditions. It is a way of reaching for an absolute reality that is independent of the outer, relative world we live in. I believe this faculty is what Carl Jung called "syncrhonicity." Others have called it common sense, intuition, conscience or right brain thinking, but the name really isn't so important. What is important is the recognition that this faculty leads to the creation of democracy and it is the only factor that can secure its survival. I think our democratic societies should make a much greater effort to identify and understand this faculty in our psyche, because it could open up many new possibilities for us.

I would like to call this faculty the "discriminating self," since it allows us to discriminate between right and wrong according to timeless principles. It is important to realize that the discriminating self is a reality—we all have one. The proof is our democratic societies. Since we have created societies based on timeless principles, we must have a faculty in our psyche that allows us to recognize these principles.

Since the intellect and emotions are functioning in a relative world, they can be both constructive and destructive. To keep them constructive we must balance them with our discriminating self, otherwise we will inevitably become ego-centered. The discriminating self and the ego are the two opposing forces that are engaged in a tug-of-war in our psyche. So, our next step is to consider the ego.

How the Ego Works

For anyone who wants a more detailed description than I am giving here, I highly recommend M. Scott Peck's book, *People of the Lie*. The book is an attempt to establish a foundation for a scientific approach to the issue of human evil. In my opinion the most important contribution of the book is that it very clearly demonstrates how the origin of the human ego is a lie. I think we should examine where this lie comes from.

Most (if not all) human actions originate from a desire; we feel a need and we act to fulfill it. The desire is an impulse and it will turn on the emotions. Our emotions will then begin to build up steam until we have the necessary energy to act on the desire. When a certain pressure is built up, the intellect becomes activated and it begins to evaluate how the desire can be fulfilled. It is important to recognize that the emotions are unable to discriminate between right and wrong desires, they cannot even fathom the term. The emotions will act blindly upon any impulse they receive.

The intellect does not evaluate the desire itself and neither does it seek to discriminate between right and wrong means for fulfilling the desire. It will seek to find the most direct course of action that leads to a fulfillment of the desire and it only discriminates between what is possible and what is not. The emotions and the intellect will act almost mechanically upon any impulse fed into them. What prevents us from being robots is the discriminating self which has the ability, and the responsibility, for evaluating desires before they are turned into action. This evaluation will be based on timeless principles and on what is enlightened self-interest. Ideally only right desires, and only desires that it is possible to fulfill, should be turned into action. In that case, the vast majority of our desires would be fulfilled and happiness would be the result.

Unfortunately most of us do not function according to this ideal scenario. What we experience is that we do not always have a direct and conscious connection to our discriminating self, we have lost the clear vision of timeless principles. One of the effects of this is that most of us are not consciously aware of many of our desires; they have been literally programmed into our subconscious minds. The result is that the emotions and the intellect are acting upon desires that are not principle-centered. Since the emotions and the intellect are unable to evaluate this, they treat all desires the same.

The emotions work like a steam engine, if too much pressure is created then it must either be released or the engine will blow up. So, when the pressure has been built up, the intellect must find a way to release it. Since the intellect operates in a relative world, it can find means to fulfill almost any desire. Unfortunately, a desire that is not principle-centered to begin with most often cannot be fulfilled through principle-centered means.

If the intellect suggests a course of action which we have been brought up to see as wrong, then we may consciously override the intellect. Since the desire cannot be fulfilled, we now have a dangerous situation because the emotions will keep building up steam. There are three possible ways out.

Ideally the discriminating self should kick in at this point which would allow us to analyze and evaluate our desire consciously. We would then realize that emotional energy is as neutral as electricity. Just as electrical energy will work in a white or a blue light bulb; emotional energy will support any desire. It is therefore possible for us to redirect our emotional energy into a more constructive desire; we can replace an ego-centered desire with a principle-centered one. The ability to do this consciously, is the difference between people who are in control of their own psyche and people who are being controlled by forces they are not aware of. Unfortunately most of us don't have this understanding and we also lack the realization that a principle is the only tool that allows us to be in control. As a result, we often take a less ideal way out.

Most of us will from time to time use our willpower to suppress the desire by seeking to force it away from our conscious minds. This does not stop the buildup of emotional energy and eventually the pressure becomes so great, that is must be released. In extreme cases this can lead to nervous breakdown, but more commonly it results in mood swings, temper tantrums, or more violent outbursts of anger.

Finally, we have a third way to release emotional energies and it is the one that gives rise to the ego. If we refuse to follow one of the suggestions of the intellect, it will immediately begin to look for another one. We may have overruled the intellect because of a principle, but the intellect cannot accept this as a reason to discard the desire. If emotional energy keeps building, the intellect will look for the most direct way to release it. After all, the intellect can only see the principle as a relative thing and thus it can easily find arguments against it. It can quickly define circumstances under which it becomes perfectly justified to disregard the principle. This can cause the ultimate seduction in which we begin to believe that what we want to do is not a violation of principles after all. Or we reason that the violation of principles is acceptable in our particular situation and therefore it will not produce any negative consequences. We may feel that even if it does produce consequences, it will still be worth it. Or we may decide that we are not going to allow principles to restrict us because that could cause a harmful emotional explosion. There is an almost infinite number of "excuses" for violating principles, but they are all based on a lie, the lie that our short-term desires are more important than our long-term interests.

Once we have begun to accept this way of reasoning, we become entrapped by it and a downward spiral begins. The first step is a need for self-justification and here the intellect is the best friend we can have. Since it can only see right and wrong as opposites on a relative scale, the intellect can justify absolutely anything. This explains why two people can hold opposite positions on an issue and both feel their opinions are justified.

After a while this process will gradually lead to the creation of a separate entity within our psyche, and it will begin to take on a life and a will of its own. I believe this is what Carl Jung called "the shadow." Others have called it the not-self, the carnal mind, the Cain consciousness or the dweller-on-the-threshold, but I prefer to call it the ego. Once the ego has been created, it will seek to expand its influence and it can become a very dominating force in our psyche. The ego can only survive as long as it can justify its own existence and make our conscious minds believe we need it. This need for ego-justification will often become a very aggressive attempt to influence other people. The ultimate justification for the ego is to make all other people agree with it. The reasoning is that if everybody else agrees with me, I must be right.

Since the ego is based on a lie, an illusion, it must constantly defend itself against anything that contradicts the lie. Thus, a person using principles to confront the ego will be seen as an enemy and will often be dealt with in a very aggressive manner. Scott Peck points out that the more ego-centered people become, the more aggressively they seek to defend their actions and opinions. They basically lose personal freedom because all their attention and energy becomes directed towards defending an illusion that they are completely unable to see.

I think we should be honest and admit that the vast majority of us have an ego and that it partially controls our opinions and actions. When we act upon ego-centered desires, two things can happen. Some of our desires cannot be fulfilled because they were unrealistic to begin with, or our actions produce unwanted consequences that prevent the fulfillment of other desires. As a result, we will have a build-up of emotional energy forcing us into doing things just to blow off steam. Instead of seeking to fulfill long-term desires, most of our energy is spent on releasing pressure so we don't blow up. Our unfulfilled desires become a giant snowball rolling behind us and we have to keep running faster to avoid being crushed by it.

I believe most of the original spiritual teachings found in the major world religions, as well as modern self-help literature, makes the point that the only key to personal happiness is to escape this downward ego-spiral. They also demonstrate that the only way to do so is to analyze our desires consciously and adjust them according to a set of principles that did not originate in the human ego. The ego tends to form a maze, a veil of energy, around us and the only way out is to follow a guideline that is not part of the maze. We could say that the only way to reach true personal happiness is to engage in a path that leads us to a higher level of awareness. We must sharpen our ability to see through the illusion of the ego, so we can escape the influence of the ego and integrate with a higher part of our being.

The Human Ego and the Abortion Debate

When we consider the intense emotions of anger and hostility that can be found in some pro-life and pro-choice proponents, I think it is rather obvious that the abortion debate has caused many people to become ego-centered at least concerning this issue. The abortion debate has been monopolized by the pro-life and pro-choice movements and they have created a win-loose situation. I believe most people think that the only possible outcome is that one of the two movements will be successful in having its position turned into a permanent law. I also believe most people will agree that no matter what kind of law society enacts, it will not end the conflict. If Roe v. Wade is overturned and abortion becomes illegal, it will in no way be a peaceful resolution. It seems like the abortion debate has lead to a gridlock, a "damned if you do and damned if you don't" situation from which there is seemingly no way out. Stephen Covey points out that ego-centered interactions will lead to a win-loose situation in which everyone eventually becomes a looser. I think that describes the present abortion debate quite accurately.

Is there a way out? I think so and in order to describe it I would like to briefly tell the story of the Gordian knot. In the third century B.C. the Greek King, Gordius decided to dedicate his wagon to Zeus and he tied the yoke and the axletree together with a very intricate knot. An oracle then prophesied that whoever could undo (note that he did not say "untie") the knot would become ruler over all of Asia. For centuries some of the wisest and most ambitious of men tried to untie the knot, but none suceeeded. Then the King of Macedonia came along and he undid the knot by cutting it with his sword, whereafter he conquered all of Asia and became known as Alexander the Great. Today "cutting the Gordian knot" symbolizes an unusual and perhaps impractical way to solve problems. I disagree! I think Alexander demonstrated the most fundamental principle for problem solving we will ever find. Simply stated, "It is impossible to solve a problem with the same state of consciousness that created it!"

If a problem is the result of an ego-centered way of thinking, then it is in reality based on an illusion created by the human intellect. How can we hope to solve the problem as long as we remain in that same state of illusion? The only possible solution is to step outside the illusion and look at the problem with a new and higher understanding. The only way to solve problems that originate in an ego-centered state of mind is to become principle-centered, because principles are the only guidelines that reach beyond the ego.

False Motives, False Ideas

In my opinion the basis for effective problem solving is the realization that the human ego has created a number of motives that are not in our enlightened self-interest. These motives are not principle-centered, so let's call them false motives.

The ego must then get the intellect to come up with a number of ideas to justify the false motives and the continued existence of the ego. It seems logical to label these as false ideas. I think we need to recognize that some of these false ideas could have been around for so long that they have literally become a part of the very fabric of our mental process. As a result they can have a very profound influence upon our society and its institutions. If we want to understand our present society as well as the events of history, we need to consider the influence of false motives and false ideas.

The extreme outcome of this interplay of the human ego and the intellect is the idea called "humanism." This philosophy defines man as the center of the universe. He has the supreme authority to define his own world according to the ideas that he chooses to accept right now. In other words, there is no such thing as an absolute principle; everything is relative to man and his beliefs. Some humanists even go so far as to say that things really do not exist until they are described and defined by man. It is only through our consciousness that they assume a reality.

It should be relatively easy to see that humanism is the all-time favorite of manipulators. No philosophy could ever be better for those who want to dominate other people. If everything is relative and defined according to human beliefs or interests, then whoever is the most shrewd intellectually automatically gets to be in a superior class. They can define a society exactly the way they want it. If we compared this with the array of philosophical systems we know, we would see that a substantial part of our political and even religious philosophies contains a disguised form of humanism.

I want to point out that I do not believe that becoming principle-centered will automatically give us the solution to all of our problems. The situations we face on planet earth today are very complex and I don't think it is possible to find "one solution to all problems" as many self-styled gurus have proclaimed. Neither do I think a principle-centered debate on abortion will automatically lead to one specific outcome. The abortion issue involves many complex elements and I don't think there is an easy solution. This book should not be seen as an attempt to promote "the one and only solution."

It is important for us to realize that it will be a very difficult process to disentangle ourselves from the ego because the motives and the reasonings of the ego are so very subtle. In order to see through the many layers of illusion we will literally have to acquire a superhuman ability to discriminate. It will also be a very painful process because is will mean the death of the ego. The ego will resist this for all it is worth and insofar as we have come to identify with the ego or its ideas, we will experience pain. I believe it is very important to realize that giving up an old, limiting paradigm will quite often cause us pain, as described in M. Scott Peck's book, *The Road Less Traveled*. The reason being that a paradigm can become part of what gives us a sense of personal identity and security. That is why it can be very difficult for us to change our opinions and why we often see a challenge of our viewpoints as a threat to our personal identity. Once the pain of letting go of an old paradigm has faded, it will give way for a new sense of personal freedom and I believe this personal growth, as well as the growth of society, is well worth the effort and pain involved.

We need to realize that all of us have an ego and all of us have false beliefs that we need to give up in order to grow. Instead of seeing people with a different opinion as enemies, we need to show compassion for them as well as for ourselves.

This understanding is the only element I see that can allow

us to depersonalize the abortion debate and free ourselves from the heavy burden of emotional energy that has been built up for two decades. Instead of fighting other people, we realize we must begin to fight the false motives and false ideas. There is more to a human being than opinions; and people can actually change their motives and beliefs. Instead of acting as if the only way to win a debate is to destroy people with different opinions, we must now take a new approach. We can expose false motives and ideas and seek to present a higher understanding of the issue that will give our opponents a positive motivation for reconsidering their position. Instead of making other people our enemies, we must fight against false ideas.

Maybe this could lead us to see that even though we may have different opinions right now; there could be a common ground. Perhaps we might even realize that most of us have a common goal. The bottom line being that we are all students walking the same path towards a higher understanding of what life is all about.

It should be obvious that all paradigms are not automatically ego-centered. A paradigm is simply a platform for our attitude towards life or a certain aspect of life. It may very well be influenced by false motives and false ideas, but it need not be. Ideally, a paradigm should not be a permanent thing, in the process of personal growth we will continually seek to refine and expand our paradigms. However, sometimes we will refuse to let go of a paradigm, usually because it gives us a sense of security. In that case even a principle-centered paradigm will become a hindrance for personal growth. So, the real test of ego-centeredness is our willingness to let go of old limitations in order to grow. The essence of the ego is a resistance to growth. I would like to propose the concept of an "ego-trap" which is simply a paradigm that we stubbornly hold on to even when it limits our personal growth.

How do we begin the process of making the abortion debate more principle-centered? I believe we should start by considering what has given rise to the pro-life and the pro-choice positions. Did certain paradigms form the basis for the evolution of the two movements and were they influenced by false motives and ideas?

PART TWO

The Paradigms

Religion and Science

CHAPTER 3

The Orthodox Christian Paradigm

Our current news-media tends to provide a fragmented picture of reality. A newspaper contains a number of short articles, each one focusing on one particular subject without putting it in a larger context. The evening news on television devotes a couple of minutes to each issue, but rarely seeks to tie the issues together. As a result we often lose the big picture which can prevent us from understanding the causes behind the effects we see in the headlines.

The majority of the media treats the abortion debate as an isolated phenomenon with no connection to other tendencies in society, but can this really give us a complete understanding of the issue? How does the abortion debate relate to certain aspects of other national debates? Is it a reflection of the consciousness of the people? Could this lack of resolution be a sign that there is an unresolved conflict in the minds of the people—a symptom showing us there is a deeper problem that we have not yet seen, or recognized for what it truly is? Are the pro-life and pro-choice movements only promoting a certain position on abortion or are they in reality promoting two different attitudes towards life, two basic paradigms? Could the two movements be the result of a battle between these paradigms?

I want to make it very clear that I am fully aware that both the pro-life and the pro-choice movements are very diversified, with people from all walks of life. I also realize that when we analyze other people's opinions and motives it is very easy to generalize and oversimplify. But, on the other hand, the only way to understand an issue is to isolate the basic elements of it, and to do that we have to look for general tendencies. So, please bear in mind that the following is not an attempt to state a universal truth that is valid for all the people involved with the two movements. It is an attempt to point to a general tendency so we can relate the abortion debate to other tendencies in society.

The pro-life position states that abortion is wrong, but what is the reasoning behind it? I think it is fair to say that most of the people holding a pro-life position believe that an abortion does kill a human person. I think it is also safe to say that for many people this position is a consequence of their religious beliefs. Many religions teach that every human being is endowed with what is most often called a soul and this soul is what makes us different from animals. Although the soul is not a product of the physical body, it is present from the moment of conception and consequently life begins at conception. So, I think we can say that a religious approach to life is one of the basic paradigms behind the pro-life position.

According to the pro-choice position, abortion is not wrong. Part of the reasoning behind this is that a fetus has not yet become a person and thus abortion does not kill a human being. I believe it is safe to say that many of the people holding this position believe human beings are the result of an evolutionary process. This evolution was first described by Charles Darwin and from the beginning until today most of its supporters have been members of the scientific community or people with a predominantly scientific attitude towards life. According to many scientists, our mental and emotional processes are the product of chemical reactions in the physical brain, thus we do not have a soul that can exist independently of the body.

I know that pro-choice people come from many different backgrounds, but I still think we can say that a scientific approach to life is one of the basic paradigms behind the pro-choice position. If we can agree that the pro-life movement is influenced by a religious paradigm and the pro-choice movement by a scientific paradigm, then we can take the next step.

By looking at history we realize that in the Western world there has, for 3-400 years, been a conflict between people espousing these two paradigms. We could literally say that there has been a war between religion and science. This is an important observation because it makes us realize that we cannot hope to understand and resolve the abortion debate unless we examine the basic paradigms. So, let us take a closer look at religion and science.

The Origin of Orthodox Christianity

Mankind has always been on a quest to answer what we call the fundamental questions of life. There are two ways to do this. We can direct our attention outward or inward. We can observe the world around us and seek to find basic principles for how the world we live in works and how it originated. This is the method applied by science. The second option is to go within and seek to establish a contact with an inner reality, giving us a direct experience of a higher source of knowledge. This is what we call a mystical, spiritual, or religious experience.

Looking at history we see that all the world's major religions originated from the second approach. One person directed the attention inward and established a direct contact with a higher level of existence. This leader became the connecting link between the people and the higher level of reality. Through the teacher, "someone" on a higher level was able to give forth an explanation of the basic questions of life. The teaching was formulated in a way that was adapted to the society and time in which it was given. Part of the teaching was a set of guidelines describing how it was possible for others to obtain the same experience as the leader. This should ideally make it possible for all to confirm the reality of the religious teaching through personal experience.

Here is an important point. If we desire to be strictly objective, we cannot rule out the possibility that there could be a higher level of reality that could only be contacted through a direct inner experience. Until one has had this inner experience, the reality of the higher level of existence can neither be proven nor disproven. Unless and until people have applied the religious teaching and made the inner contact themselves, the acceptance of the leader and his teaching will rest solely on faith.

Modern science is the result of the outgoing approach.

Through our observations of the world we live in, we seek to formulate a concept of what life is and how it originated. This is what Darwin, and many others with him, sought to do with the theory of the origin of species. Again, if we desire to be strictly objective, we must say that science is based on what we know and have observed. We cannot rule out the existence of a level of reality that we have not yet discovered, in fact, science has repeatedly revealed still deeper layers of the material world. Neither can we rule out that there could be levels of existence that we cannot discover through material science.

Therefore, when people take the position that modern science has given a complete explanation of the reality of life, this position must be based on faith. It is the same kind of faith held by religious people who have not had an inner, personal experience.

Most people who hold a religious position believe in the existence of something they have not personally experienced. Most people who hold a scientific position believe in the non-existence of something they have not personally experienced. For both kinds of people, it can be said that their position is solely a matter of faith. We are all believers; the only difference is what we believe in, which leads us to consider what sparks faith.

What Is Faith?

According to the dictionary, faith is an unquestioning belief in something. Without going into a deeper psychological discussion, we can say that faith is a very individual matter. When it comes to ideas that seek to explain the fundamental questions of life, people will only accept a given idea if it seems plausible to them. Each person has an individual standard, or measuring rod, for evaluating an idea. This standard may be somewhat changeable, however, and most people find that over the course of a lifetime their standard becomes refined, it matures. If we look at society in a historical context, we will see that there is a constant process of change in people's beliefs. In our Western nations, we have, over the past 2,000 years, seen a major change concerning people's faith. It started when the majority of the population had faith in the Judeo-Christian tradition and felt it gave plausible answers to the fundamental questions of life. Today this has changed. Although many people still hold onto the Christian tradition, it seems that a large part of the people believe modern science offers more plausible answers to at least some of the fundamental questions. Why has this change occurred? To make it easier to answer this broad question, let us focus on a more specific question: Has something happened to the Christian message over the centuries that has made the explanation of the fundamental questions of life seem less believable to the people of today?

The Christian faith started out like all other major religions. One person—in this case, Jesus—developed a state of consciousness that enabled him to bridge the gap between our normal, conscious awareness and a higher level of reality. He became the open door through which a new and higher spiritual understanding was given to us. Although Jesus's message was based on the existing religious tradition, it did in some ways conflict with this tradition and introduced many new concepts. Thus, Jesus became a threat to the established power structure of his time, and consequently, he was dealt with the same way an established power elite always deals with a dangerous individual.

Today, the heart and soul of Christianity is still the message given by Jesus. For two millennia, no new teaching from above has been added to the original teachings. The question is, how much of the original message has survived the ravages of time?

This question requires almost a lifetime of study, but let us look at a representative selection of the many possible options:

1. The scriptures, as we know them today, are focused on the three years of Jesus's life between the age of 30 and his crucifixion. There is no record in the Bible of his life between the ages of 12 and 29. The heart of the Christian faith is that the individual lifestream of Jesus did not die with his physical body but appeared again after his resurrection. According to a second-century tradition Jesus taught his disciples for 10 to 20 years after his resurrection, but there are no records of what he taught them.

2. The New Testament records very little of the teachings of Jesus in his own words. John 21:25 states

that if everything Jesus did and spoke should be written down, the world could not contain the books that should be written. How much of the original teaching was never written down and remain unavailable to us? Can we truly say that the scriptures we have today give a comprehensive picture of Jesus's direct words?

3. Several scriptural passages allude to the fact that Jesus gave his teachings on two different levels. He taught the multitudes in parables, but when he was alone with his disciples, he expounded all things to them. Most religions have an outer and inner (exoteric and esoteric) teaching and Christianity is no exception. In the second to third century A.D., Clement of Alexandria wrote about a secret Gospel of Mark intended only for people who were being initiated into the inner mysteries of the Christian faith. This gospel apparently disappeared. We cannot know how many other esoteric teachings have disappeared or were never written down.

4. Biblical scholars agree that the gospels we have today cannot be considered completely accurate. It is generally assumed that the gospels were not written down until 70–100 years after the crucifixion. Many inaccuracies can be traced to scribal errors, or errors in the translations. It is a fact that we have thousands of manuscripts that differ in more than 250,000 ways. In fact, there is not one single sentence in the gospels for which the tradition is entirely uniform.

5. During the first centuries, the Orthodox Church suppressed or willfully destroyed many of the early Gnostic writings, those that they believed to be heretic. This happened during the process of setting the canon. In the fourth century, the Archbishop Athanasius decreed that all books reflecting ideas considered anathema (accursed) should be burned.

6. In A.D. 543, the Byzantine Emperor Justinian I was instrumental in having a great number of early Christian writings, and even certain ideas, anathemized at a church council in Constantinople. In 553, Justinian

called the entire Catholic Church to the fifth Ecumenical Council, in which almost all bishops of the Eastern church attended. This council confirmed the earlier anathemas, but the Pope was not present and there is no record of papal approval. Therefore, some scholars question the legitimacy of the anathemas. Nevertheless, later church councils have affirmed the anathemas, and today most Christian churches still uphold the banning of many early writings and the ideas expressed in them. In reality, this means that for the past 1,500 years, the orthodox Christian churches have held the position that there are certain ideas that no Christian is allowed to think, talk or write about.

On the basis of these facts, we can make two observations:

   1. We do not have a complete record of what Jesus taught. We do not know the entirety of his teachings, nor the full scope of his inner message. If an idea is not described in the scriptures as we know them today, it could still be part of the complete teachings of Jesus. It appears that historical facts compel us to be flexible rather than rigid in our approach to Christianity.

   2. Scholars show us that the message of the Christian faith has been willfully tampered with, which prompts us to ask who did it, what was their motive and how has it affected our civilization?

The Church and the Human Ego

We earlier described how the human ego works in creating false motives and false ideas. It is important to realize that when an original religious teaching is given, it does not originate in the human ego, but comes from a level of reality that is beyond the ego. Therefore, all true religious teachings can serve as guidelines that will allow us to create a principle-centered society. In fact, the main purpose for religion may be to assist us in liberating ourselves from the chains of the ego. However, as soon as we no longer have a direct contact with a higher level of reality (progressive revelation), it is inevitable that the original teachings will become the subject of interpretation.

What happens if this interpretation is influenced by persons with ego-centered motives? Could this cause the original message to become diluted or even lost? Is it possible that this process could have influenced the evolution of the Christian Church? It is obvious that Jesus was a threat to the power elite of his time and that they sought to kill not only him but his message. It is commonly known that in the first centuries, Christians were persecuted wherever they went. Still the faith persisted and an organized church was formed. Is it possible that the organization of the Christian church was influenced by ego-centered people and if so how could it have affected the content of the teaching?

In the first centuries, the Christian faith was extremely diversified, with many different groups espousing a variety of beliefs. Gradually, these diversified groups were suppressed by the emergence of an orthodox church with a centralized organizational structure. This centralization culminated in the formation of the Roman Catholic Church in the fourth century. Regardless of the diversity in the early church, there were two main tendencies fighting for dominion. One was the belief that the core of Christianity was a path of personal initiation under Jesus, with personal works, faith and grace all being part of the road to salvation. This belief was held by, among others, the Gnostics, who represented a challenge to the Orthodox church. According to orthodoxy, the only road to salvation was through faith, which means that a person could only receive salvation through the church and its hierarchy of the priesthood ruled by the Pope. When the Roman Emperor Constantine converted to Christianity in the fourth century, the Orthodox church succeeded in suppressing virtually everyone they had labelled as heretics—among them, the Gnostics.

A number of Gnostic texts were discovered at Nag Hamadhi, Egypt in 1945. These texts are the subject of the book *The Gnostic Gospels* by Elaine Pagels. She writes that the Orthodox church succeeded in establishing a hierarchy of persons through whom all others had to approach God. The Gnostic idea of a personal path of initiation was in opposition to the church hierarchy and the Orthodox church did all in its power to suppress it. When orthodoxy gained military support after the conversion of Constantine, the penalty for heresy escalated dramatically. Whereas the bishops had earlier been victimized by the police, they were now put in command of the police and used their new power to suppress anyone with divergent beliefs. Possession of books denounced as heretic was made a criminal offense, and all such books were destroyed.

What this boils down to is simply mind control. The Orthodox church defined what people were allowed to think, and they used all means to make people conform to doctrine. This demonstrated a complete lack of respect for individual freedom and a desire to confine the people into a very narrow outer framework. I think most of us can agree that this was hardly a principle-centered way to do things.

How has the suppression of some of these early Christian ideas affected our civilization?

When it comes to explaining the reality of human existence, we can take two approaches:

1. The identity of the individual is inseparably linked to the physical body. The individual has no existence before the conception or birth of the body, nor does he or she live on independently after the death of the body. According to traditional Christianity, the soul may be saved and receive eternal life in some kind of higher sphere after its earthly life. This salvation is determined by faith alone. If the soul is not saved at the end of this life, it is presumably snuffed out of existence. There are different ways to formulate this concept, but what they all boil down to is that life and salvation are one-shot deals.

2. The identity of the individual has an existence that is independent of the physical body. It exists before the conception of the body and it will continue to exist when the body dies. If the soul has not qualified for salvation after one lifetime, it may be given another chance—or several, as required. The soul is the true identity of a person, whereas the body is merely a temporary physical vehicle through which the soul is expressing itself in the physical world. The salvation of the soul depends not only on faith and grace but also on how the soul has made use of its opportunity in this life. There are different ways to formulate this concept, but what they all say is that life is a continuum.

Removing the Inner Teaching?

History shows us that the second approach was banned as heresy by the early Christian church. It also shows us that it was done not so much for theological purposes, but for political purposes.

The Christian church was extremely apocalyptic during the first century. The Second Coming of Christ was expected any day, and when he appeared, this world would be rolled up like a scroll to give way for a better world. When you believe the world may come to an end tomorrow, it becomes less interesting to consider life as a continuum. As time and the world went on, the interest in life as a continuum increased, but only outside orthodox circles. The reason it did not appeal to orthodoxy was purely political. The fact is that the idea of life as a continuum was a threat to the established hierarchy of the church. The early church fathers had a very strong belief that the church as an organization was indispensable to Christian salvation. In other words, people could only be saved through the church hierarchy. Its priests were mediators of God's grace channeled to people through the sacraments, which the clergy controlled. The belief in life as a continuum granted so much autonomy and authority to the individual that it could lead to the belief that the church was not indispensable to the individual's salvation. This had a potential for undermining centralized authority. The very basis for the Roman Catholic Church was the idea that centralized authority was critical to the survival of Christianity (which shows how much the philosophy of the Roman Empire, in which the emperor was seen as the only representative of God on earth, affected the creation of the Church). Seeing life as a continuum would put the emphasis on individual free will and personal accountability instead of defining church hierarchy as the only road to God.

The best way to gain control over others is to set up a barrier between their conscious awareness and the absolute level of existence. We could put it this way: You must make people believe that the only way to God is through an earthly authority. If people can approach God directly and individually, it becomes very difficult for an earthly authority to control them.

The fifth Ecumenical Council stated: "If anyone asserts the fabulous preexistence of souls and shall assert the monstrous restoration which follows from it, let him be anathema!"

Anathema means *cursed.* If you dared to think about life as a continuum, you would have the curse of the Church upon you. Then the Church would make sure you could not enter heaven. Is it any wonder that the idea of life as a continuum eventually disappeared from our Western civilization? Maybe not, but it most certainly is a wonder that this curse, defined by a handful of power-hungry church fathers, has been upheld by the majority of Christian churches until the present day!

As we said earlier, there are no records showing papal approval of the fifth Ecumenical Council. Thus, some scholars claim that the church's rejection of the idea of life as a continuum is not based on a basic incompatibility with the gospel, but on incompatibility with patristic theory. Consequently, nothing prevents the reconsideration of this idea today. For more information on this, see *Reincarnation for the Christian,* by Quincy Howe. Some scholars claim the gospels contain passages that suggest that Jesus either taught or was familiar with the idea of the continuity of life. As was mentioned earlier, we have no way of knowing if Jesus taught this idea as part of his inner teaching, which was never recorded. What we do know for certain is that with the appearance of the Roman Catholic Church, the idea of life as a continuum was willfully removed from Western thought. We must consider how this has affected our civilization.

Fundamental Questions Without Answers

We have to realize that the idea of life as a continuum has been a part of mankind's philosophical and religious teachings from time immemorial. Most of the world's religions teach that life is a continuum; many past civilizations believed in it, as do many cultures of today. Actually, a majority of the world's population believes in the continuity of life in one form or another. Polls have shown that between one half and two thirds of all Americans believe in this idea. It is therefore safe to say that the idea of life as a continuum was part of mankind's consciousness in the early days of Christianity. So what happened when the Roman Church clamped down on the idea and sought to eradicate it from the third to the sixth century?

For at least some people, the idea of life as a continuum is and always has been the only way to find plausible answers to some of the fundamental questions of life. It is only through this idea that their faith is sparked. They simply cannot find plausible answers by seeing life as a one-shot deal. When the idea of continuity was removed from Christian thought, it is possible that the Christian faith was deprived of a spiritual element that for some people was the very thing that sparked their faith. In other words, Christianity lost its appeal to some people, and their faith either faded away or was turned into a rote, outer, intellectual acceptance.

During the Middle Ages, the Roman Catholic Church assumed the role of an extremely powerful political factor, with enormous influence on society and people's ways of thinking. The Church maintained its tendency to exercise mind control and rigidly stuck to ideas that today are clearly seen as superstitious, such as the belief that the earth is flat. Why did the Church become so rigid in its approach to the fundamental questions of life? Was it because there was no longer any plausible way to answer these questions within official doctrine? Even today, most Christian churches cannot give plausible answers to many of these questions. The common answer is "It's a mystery," which contains the subtle suggestion that we are not supposed to know certain things about life. Many people have experienced how the churches fail to give answers and manage to make people feel they are asking inappropriate questions. For an orthodox person, any question that cannot be readily answered by official doctrine is automatically considered inappropriate and it has always been that way. But we are talking about questions that mankind has been asking since the earliest civilizations. How can such fundamental questions suddenly become inappropriate? Did the reality of life change when the Roman Church was organized? Or is the answer that the Orthodox church gradually became more ego-centered? (For a detailed explanation of why churches tend to become rigid, see *When God Becomes a Drug* by Father Leo Booth)

Take note of what really happened in this process. Jesus gave us the Christian faith through his own inner experiences, and he told us to go and do likewise. Many early Christians encouraged this individual approach to God, but the Orthodox church sought to put an end to it. What the Orthodox church did was to put a barrier between the individual and the absolute level of existence. Many saints have been able to cross that barrier and gain the direct, inner experience anyway, but the majority of the people have not been able to do so. In other words, when the Christian faith was organized, the Orthodox church lost its direct contact to the absolute level of existence. So instead of having a direct link beyond the relative world, the Church became confined, or confined itself, to existing doctrine. That could be why we have not had a progressive revelation bringing forth new teachings in the Christian faith; the Orthodox church closed the door to it. In a sense, orthodox doctrine has aborted the direct inner experience that has always been the very core of religious life. We could ask if there is any meaning to religion without this experience? And, is the loss of this element the reason Christianity has lost its appeal to a large part of the population?

If the direct inner experience is lost, what is left, but blind obedience to an outer doctrine?

CHAPTER 4

The Scientific Paradigm

The Birth of Science

In the Middle Ages, when superstition was at its peak, a new tendency in human thought emerged, and it has culminated in modern science. It is important to look at the situation that led to the emergence of science. The Catholic church of the time rigidly enforced the belief that the earth was flat and the center of the universe with the sun and all the planets revolving around it. In several European nations the Church also carried out the execution of a great number of alleged witches. These women were basically what we today would call "holistic health-practitioners." In at least some nations the process devised by the church for exposing a witch was as follows: If someone had raised suspicion against a woman, she would be thrown into a lake or pond. If she managed to float on top, she was a witch and would then be burned alive. If she sank to the bottom, she was innocent, and then it was just too bad. The kings of the time were just as superstitious and I think we can say that ego-centeredness had become institutionalized by both Church and State. In this situation it is no wonder that some people were seeking for a way out of the maze of the human ego. The solution was introduced by Francis Bacon as the scientific method. The essence of this method is that we always test the accuracy of our theories through repeated experiments.

Considering how the medieval churches operated, it is probably no wonder that this lead some people to abandon the spiritual or religious tradition as useless or even dangerous. We have to ask if this came about because the Christian faith had lost its plausibility? Was it because the idea of the continuity of life and other ideas had been removed, that the Western civilization started to turn away from a spiritual approach to life? If this is the case, then we must conclude that the crucial decisions made by a small body of church fathers some 1,400 years ago set the stage for the present abortion debate. Therefore, these decisions could be the real cause behind our society's inability to find a resolution to the question of abortion (more about that later).

The Mechanistic Science

The scientific revolution made its major breakthrough when Isaac Newton formulated the laws of gravity and motion. Building upon his foundation a number of scientists developed what we can call a materialistic, mechanistic and deterministic science.

In the late 1800's most scientists seriously believed they had discovered virtually everything there was to discover and that, except for a few minor details, they could explain it all in terms of mechanical laws. According to their scientific paradigm, the universe could be likened to a huge machine and we where simply cogs in the clockwork of creation. This paradigm was based on what we can perceive with our senses and measure with scientific instruments. It was believed that everything in the universe followed the mechanical laws described by Newton and consequently everything could be predicted. If we knew enough about the present conditions of a particle or a planetary system, the mechanical laws would enable us to predict its future behavior. According to this model a human being is also bound by deterministic laws and all notion of free will is an illusion. The mechanistic science caused many people to label all phenomenon that could not be measured by scientific instruments as unreal. Ideas such as free will, the soul, spiritual purpose, higher beings and God came to be seen as the result of pure superstition

It is important for us to understand that the mechanistic world view is very much at the root of our official paradigms today. For the last hundred years this model has found its way into all aspects of our society. Most people in the Western world were brought up to accept a mechanistic paradigm and it had a very profound effect on our way of thinking.

However, the most advanced scientists of today have completely abandoned the mechanistic, deterministic world view. In this century, and especially in the last two decades, scientists have begun formulating a new basis for science that is not deterministic. This development began in 1905 when Albert Einstein shook the foundations of Newtonian science with the theory of relativity. According to Newtonian science, the universe is built from two separate components, matter and energy. With his famous formula Einstein proved that matter is simply another form of energy. What we see and measure is a manifestation of something that we cannot see and that we may not even be able to measure with the best instruments. In other words, the material universe is an expression of a more subtle or more fundamental level of existence. This is basically what all the major religions have been saying for thousands of years.

The theory of relativity also states that our observations of the laws of physics will depend on the frame of reference from which we observe. Unless we take this into account, we cannot make reliable observations of the universe. Einstein was thus the first person to prove that unless we consider how our observations are affected by our paradigms, we can never know reality.

In the 1920s a number of scientists used Einstein's theories as the foundation for the development of a new branch of science called quantum mechanics. It deals with the world of subatomic particles such as electrons, protons, neutrons and even smaller particles. Quantum mechanics completely shattered the remnants of deterministic science. There are three elements in this process.

1. It has been proven through numerous experiments that it is impossible to predict the behavior of a subatomic particle. The reason is not that we do not know enough about the present condition of the particle, but that the subatomic world does not follow deterministic laws. All scientists agree on this point. Some scientists believe there is an element of free will involved with the behavior of subatomic particles although no one has yet been able to explain how it

works. In any event, the inescapable conclusion is that the universe is not a big machine. There is quite a bit of disagreement as to how to interpret these findings and how to relate them to other areas of the human experience. More recently, some scientists have begun to explore the relationship between matter and consciousness and they believe the universe resembles a huge mind rather than a machine. They argue that the incredibly intricate universe simply cannot be the result of mechanistic laws, but could only have been created by a mind that formed a blueprint before the actual creation began.

2. Quantum mechanics is the most elaborately documented theory in the history of science. Millions of experiments have been performed on particle accelerators all over the world confirming this theory. Many of these experiments have shown that a subatomic particle can actually appear out of nothing. Some physicists speak about a vacuum state in which the different particles exist only as potentialities. Through some unknown process one of the potentialities is transformed into an actuality and appears as a physical particle. It is an inescapable conclusion that the consciousness of an observer plays a necessary part in this process. It seems as if matter could not exist without mind.

3. According to Newtonian' science a human being can act as an independent observer who is in no way affecting the process he or she is observing. According to quantum physics this is impossible, an observer will inevitably become a part of the observed system. In fact our consciousness is a necessary ingredient in any observation. Some physicists believe that the subatomic particles would not exist as actualities unless they were observed by some kind of consciousness. According to the old science, we could step outside the physical universe and become impartial observers that were separated from the rest of creation. The new science states that we can never separate ourselves from the universe and that everything in the world is linked to everything else. What one person on earth does will affect, and be affected by, everything else

that is going on in the universe.

Now let us jump to another field of modern science, namely neurophysiology. Through a special form of brain surgery, neuroscientists have been able to create a very detailed map of the human brain showing that many of our faculties correspond to a part of the brain. However, several neurosurgeons claim to have proven that the most important faculties of the human mind, such as free will, self-consciousness and reason, do not have a physical location in the brain. In other words the faculties that set us apart from animals are not the result of chemical processes in the brain.

These findings are in total opposition to the mechanistic science which claimed that all of our mental processes where the result of physical interactions between parts of the matter universe. According to the old science, mind could not exist independently of matter nor could it influence matter.

Some scientists still hold onto the old paradigm that if we knew more about the brain, we would see all of our faculties as the result of chemical processes. But, according to the most recent discoveries in quantum physics, it is quite possible that a part of our personality, call it mind or soul, can exist independently of the physical body. The existence of such a non-material being does in no way contradict the theory of relativity or quantum mechanics.

The relationship between the brain and the mind or soul can be pictured like the relationship between a car and the driver. The car is a material object that has no consciousness or will of its own. When the driver enters, the car takes on a life-like appearance. For an observer who was unaware of the difference, it might seem as if the driver and the car were inseparable or even the same phenomenon. As long as the car is moving, the driver cannot separate him- or herself from it. But we know that the car is simply a tool that enables the driver to move from place to place. We also know that the driver can stop the car, get out, and continue an existence that is independent of the car.

If a non-material soul does exist, then it is in accord with the latest discoveries of science to reason that it could possibly survive the death of the physical body and even be in existence before birth or conception. The idea of the continuity of life is in no way contradictory to the new science. This idea might enable us to gain a new perspective on abortion.

Religion and Science Coming Together

Within the last two decades a number of modern scientists have begun to openly discuss the more philosophical aspects of quantum mechanics. Some of them have suggested that the latest theories of science contain a mystical or spiritual element that could be seen as a parallel to many of the world's religions. A few scientists have suggested that religion and science are two parallel ways of answering the fundamental questions of life and that much could be gained by trying to unify them. Science and religion could be seen as two different languages describing the same reality. If we could come up with a translator, both fields might benefit and we could open up a new world for human thought. What I have described above is a very sketchy glimpse of this process, but I hope the reader will explore some of the many popular books that makes it relatively easy for a layman to gain insight into the latest discoveries of science. Some of the most accessible of these books are: *The Tao of Physics* by Fridtjof Capra, *The Dancing Wu Li Masters* by Gary Zukav, *Quantum Reality* by Nick Herbert, *The New Story of Science* by Robert Augros and George Stanciu, *Syncrhonicity* by David Peat, *The Mind of God* by Paul Davies and a number of others. I think anyone who read these books would agree that the deterministic, mechanistic world view is dead, or at least dying.

On the basis of these observations we can draw a couple of important conclusions. Our society is still holding onto a scientific paradigm, namely the mechanistic, deterministic world view, which has been rendered obsolete by science itself. This is really nothing unusual since it often takes a while before new discoveries filter down through all the institutions of a society. In most European nations it took several decades after Columbus's discoveries before people abandoned the paradigm of a flat earth.

Nevertheless it may now be time to make a serious effort to bring society up-to-date with modern science. If we really want to find a peaceful resolution to the abortion controversy, we may wish to consider how the latest discoveries of science could bring a new element into the debate.

We can also conclude that the present abortion debate is just one battle in the war between religion and science, a war that has been going on in our minds for 400 years. When we consider the latest developments in science we can see that this war is really a battle between traditional or mechanistic science and traditional or orthodox Christianity. As we have seen above, both traditional science and traditional religion could very well be based on a limited understanding of life.

Apparently millions of Americans agree with this since the last two decades have seen a surge in the interest of alternative explanations to old questions. There is a large scale religious renewal going on in which people are seeking to reestablish a direct contact to a higher level of reality. Likewise, there is an enormous interest in the new science. Perhaps we should try to look beyond the old paradigms of religion and science to piece together a new approach to life. Perhaps such an approach could provide us with a key to resolving the abortion debate.

PART THREE

What Can We Do About the Abortion Debate?

CHAPTER 5

A New Approach to Life

For 20 years American society has been in a gridlock because of the abortion issue. Let us, in this section, try to be practical and consider how we can break the spell. What measures could be taken to bring new elements into the situation and put us on the way to a real resolution?

This book has sought to establish the idea that the debate is unresolved because it has been influenced by ideas and motives that are ego-centered, we could say that the debate is a mixture of true and false ideas.

One solution to the abortion debate would be that we recognize this mechanism and try to remove the false ideas from the debate. The problem with a false idea is that it is based on a limited understanding of life and as a result it blocks our personal growth. It is not enough to simply identify all the false ideas; we must also try to look beyond them to grasp a deeper understanding. The advantage of going beyond our old paradigms is that it opens up for an entirely new approach to life; it allows us to look at life with a new mind. Albert Einstein and many other scientists have stated that this new mind-set is the beginning of all true science. I think many spiritual writings demonstrate that it is also the beginning of all true religion.

Since I have brought up this point, I think it is reasonable that I seek to provide a sketchy outline for a new approach to life. I am fully aware that this will touch upon some of the fundamental questions of life and therefore it may easily come in conflict with people's existing beliefs. Even though many people may not be able to accept all of my suggestions, I still think a book of this type can provide a foundation for further discussion. For those, who cannot accept this chapter, I suggest a couple of more practical measures in Chapter 9.

Before I present this new approach, I would like to make it clear that I am not trying to define a new religion or a new scientific doctrine. I am not trying to present something that will replace the reader's existing beliefs and I do not intend it to be the final word on the issue. It is meant as a suggestion that points in a new direction. I hope others, whether they agree with my suggestions or not, will expand it, refine it or come up with something better. If it makes sense to you, give it further consideration, if not, simply ignore it and go on to the next chapter.

Can We Find a New Approach to Life?

In Part Two I presented the idea that the evolution of both science and religion has been influenced by ego-centered motives and that our official paradigms are a mixture of true and false ideas. I believe most of us should be able to agree on this point. I have noticed that many scientifically minded people find it very easy to see the shortcomings of religion and, likewise, many religious people see the limitations of science. The problem is that some scientifically minded people use the shortcomings of religion as an excuse for completely discarding religion and spirituality. Some religious people use essentially the same mechanism as an excuse for ignoring science. This attitude can be very limiting because it fails to recognize the real cause of the imperfections of both science and religion.

The limitations we see today really did not occur until both science and religion had become organized. An organization is run by people and it is inevitable that the organization will be influenced by the motives and beliefs of its leaders. Since motives and beliefs are processes in the human psyche, this brings us back to our discussion of the ego from Part One. What we realize is that when the ego deals with an idea, it will begin to change the original contents. Through a gradual, and sometimes very subtle process, the ego will transform a true idea into a belief system that is partially or completely false. When an organization is taken over by ego-centered people, its original goal may be partially replaced by false motives. The organization is turned into a vehicle for the ego-centered desires of its leaders.

So, what scientists see as the shortcomings of religion and what religious people see as the limitations of science, could actually be the signature of the human ego. By considering the influence of the ego, I think we can begin to makes sense out of many historical events that have so far been inexplicable. We also realize that humankind has always been engaged in a process of trying to free ourselves from the bonds of the ego by seeking for guidelines, a set of principles, that did not originate in the ego. I think that is what science and religion is all about. Through religion we seek to establish a contact to a higher level of creation and bring forth a set of principles. We could call this a spiritual approach. Through science we seek to understand the material world we live in and extract a set of principles from nature. This could be called a materialistic approach.

What I would like to propose is that these two methods are not in competition with each other, they are not mutually exclusive. It could be necessary for us to use both science and religion to gain a complete understanding of life. Is it possible that we will one day have a set of spiritual principles that have been proven through materialistic science?

One of the most exciting phenomenon in our modern culture is the budding attempts to unify science and religion. The following outline of a new approach to life is an attempt to see how the unification of scientific and religious principles could advance our understanding.

Does Life Have a Spiritual Side?

As our first step, let us consider how religion and science deal with the question of a spiritual side to life.

The basic idea behind most religions is that the physical world is the expression of a higher level of reality. The essence of this spiritual world is that it is real, but not in the same sense as the physical world. A spiritual universe is not made up of physical particles and may not be limited by time and space.

Although materialistic science denied the existence of a spiritual world, the new science is beginning to consider it as a possibility. We were all taught in school that matter is made up of molecules, which are made up of atoms made up of elementary particles. What most of us were not told is that, based on the theories of quantum mechanics, mathematical models were developed that predicted the existence of even smaller particles. A large number of these subatomic particles have been discovered through the use of particle accelerators.

What has become apparent through this new branch of science is that when we deal with the subatomic world there is a complete breakdown of the paradigms that arise from our physical senses. A so-called subatomic particle cannot be envisioned as a physical entity like a tennis ball, but rather as a vibratory action. So, what we normally call physical matter is in reality an interference pattern of different vibratory frequencies.

This has led some scientists to postulate the existence of parallel universes that exist alongside with our own. Here is one example of how we might begin to bridge the gap between religious and scientific terminology.

We know that light vibrates at a number of different frequencies, some of which are either too slow or to fast to be detected by our physical sight. We could speculate that we live in what may be called the physical octave. There could be other worlds, other octaves, that exist parallel to ours, but vibrate at frequencies that are so much slower or faster that they cannot be detected by our physical senses. Perhaps our consciousness has the capacity to bridge the gap and tune in to higher or lower octaves which could explain the age-old concepts of heaven and hell? Perhaps there is an interchange between the different octaves. When scientists say that a subatomic particle appears out of nothing, this vacuum state could be the meeting point between the physical octave and the octave immediately above it in frequency. One subatomic particle, or the entire universe, may have originated at this higher level as an idea and was then lowered into physical vibration. I am not saying that these interpretations have been proven by modern science, but they have not been disproven.

In order to avoid becoming too theoretical, let us conclude with a commonsense approach by considering what gives us a feeling of personal identity. When we say "I am," what gives us this ability to be self-conscious? Is this phenomenon of self-knowledge, which as far as we know is only found in humans, simply a matter of chemical processes in the physical brain, or is there more to it? Is there more to our personal identity than what we experience through our five senses and the intellect?

I think most people would feel appalled at being labeled a product of chemical reactions. They will object to being treated as a "thing" by others because they feel there is more to their personal identity. In other words, when we look deeply into our hearts, most of us realize that there is more to life than materialistic manifestations.

We have now come to what might be called the nexus-point of this book. Regardless of what science, religion or common sense tells us, the acceptance or non-acceptance of a spiritual side to life will always be an intimately personal decision. I am in no way trying to judge people's beliefs, I am only pointing out that people, who do not believe in spiritual aspects, will find the rest of this section rather meaningless and I recommend they go on to the next chapter. The reason being that if life is a material manifestation, then there is no basis for a further discussion about abortion; it is just another chemical process. An abortion is, in principle, no different from what happens when an acid transforms a solid object into its chemical components. It is simply a matter of an interchange of matter. The ultimate consequence of the position that life is a material manifestation is that there is no meaning whatsoever to any moral or ethical considerations. Nothing can be wrong, anything goes and the stronger will consume the weaker. We have then brought ourselves back to the law of the jungle and timeless principles really have no meaning. In that case, there would be nothing wrong with the extreme of a pro-life activist trying to kill all doctors who are performing abortions.

The fact that we acknowledge the existence of spiritual aspects, does not mean that we will agree on everything, but at least we have a basis for further discussion.

Is There a Purpose for Life?

When we say something is spiritual, what do we mean? Obviously, we mean something that is different from the material world, something that reaches beyond the physical universe. When we say we have a spiritual identity, we mean that there is a part of us that is not a product of chemical processes in the physical brain. We all know that our brains are chemical factories and that by inducing certain chemicals into the brain (such as alcohol) we will affect our thoughts and feelings. Yet, we feel there is a core of our identity that exists independently of the physical brain. If we look at the world's religions, we will see that since the beginning of time, man has believed in the existence of such a spiritual identity. It has often been called the soul or the spiritual self.

If such a spiritual self does exist, then it must, by its very nature, be able to exist independently of the physical body, or it would not be spiritual. We can therefore reason that the spiritual self will not die with the physical body, but we don't have to rely on reason since modern science has given us a helping hand. Because of advances in medical technology, thousands of people have been brought back to life after they were declared clinically dead. Many of these people experienced leaving the physical body behind and having conscious experiences in a different world. The phenomenon has been labelled "near-death experiences" and has been the subject of a number of books, some written by medical doctors. One of the most detailed and heart-warming books on the subject is Betty J. Eadie's *Embraced by the Light.* At the time I am writing this, the book is on the New York Times bestseller list which shows that a large number of people take the subject seriously.

The basis for the scientific method is that we conduct repeated experiments and, if a majority of them give the same results, then we must consider these results as reliable. A majority of the people with near-death experiences have given reports that follow the same basic patterns. So, I think we can say that there is a body of scientific evidence which suggests that part of our identity can survive the death of the physical body. Death may simply be a process in which the spiritual self disentangles itself from the physical body and goes on to live in another dimension, a spiritual world beyond the physical universe.

Now, let us turn around and look in the opposite direction. If the spiritual self does not die with the physical body, then why should it suddenly pop up out of nowhere at the birth, or even at the conception of this body? The book *Life Between Life* by Dr. Joel L. Whitton and Joe Fisher describes how people, through hypnotic regression, were able to remember conscious experiences before birth.

A large number, if not all, of the world's religions contains teachings about the existence of the "soul" before the physical body. Some Christians may not be able to accept this, but I think a closer look at the historical facts might form the basis for a reconsideration of the idea and I suggest reading the book *Reincarnation for the Christian* by Quincy Howe.

The reason the idea of a spiritual self that can exist independently of the physical body is so important, is that it can provide us with an entirely new perspective on abortion.

After more than two decades of abortion debate the central question is still, when does life begin? If we accept the idea that we have a spiritual self that can exist independently of the physical body, then we have taken a giant step towards resolving this question. By considering what life is, we may not have determined exactly when life begins, but we can see when life does not begin. If the spiritual self is not limited to the physical body then life does not begin at birth, nor does it begin at conception. If the existence of the spiritual self was in any way dependent upon the physical body, then it would not be a spiritual phenomenon. We must therefore reason that the life of every individual really began when the spiritual self, the soul, first came into being.

By acknowledging the existence of a spiritual side of life, we have, in fact, come to the point where we can answer one of the fundamental questions that has baffled us since the beginning of time, namely, "What is the purpose of life?"

If we accept that life has spiritual aspects, we are saying that there are at least two distinct levels of existence, there is a spiritual world and a material world. If we accept that the spiritual aspect of our identity, the soul, is capable of inhabiting a physical body, then we must reason that there is an interchange between the two worlds. What happens in the spiritual world will affect the physical world and vice versa. When we look at the material world we can make some basic observations. The physical universe is expanding and all living things are constantly evolving or growing. The simplest possible definition of life is that life is growth. If growth is a basic principle in the physical universe, then will the spiritual world lack growth? In other words, the spiritual self will be engaged in a process of growth in the spiritual world.

In the physical world, we think in terms of limitations, such as time and space. Our physical bodies are confined to one particular location in time and space. Since the spiritual world is different from the physical world, it is not likely that our soul will be subject to the same limitations as our body. It is not unreasonable to assume that our souls are engaged in a process of growth defined by laws governing the spiritual world. In other words, the soul could be engaged in this process before the birth and after the death of the physical body, the life of the soul being a continuum.

There are people who believe our souls can only have one chance of being in a physical body, and there are other people who believe we can have many chances. This discussion has created enormous division among religious people, but it isn't relevant in this context. Whether we have one or more chances, we can make this conclusion: The basic purpose for the life we are living right now is the growth of our soul, our spiritual self. Our physical body is a vehicle for our soul's growth and the physical universe is our schoolroom. What we learn in this life will affect whatever kind of existence our soul will have after the death of our physical body. If this is the case, our soul will have an inherent drive to make maximum use of its opportunity in this particular life. Therefore, it is likely that we have an inner longing for spiritual growth and that we will only feel completely happy when this urge is fulfilled. Could it be that the key to experiencing happiness in this physical world is to be engaged in a process that gives our souls the opportunity for spiritual growth? Could it be that when people feel their lives are empty and unfulfilled, it is because their souls are not growing spiritually? Could spiritual growth be the key to overcoming the many forms of unhappiness and frustration?

Let us take a broader look at the issue of the purpose of life.

Modern science has revealed that the existence of our universe is dependent upon a very intricate and delicate balance between the basic physical forces. If this balance was moved just a little bit in either direction, the universe would either collapse or be changed beyond recognition. Some scientists believe that such a narrow balance simply cannot be the result of chance events, but must be based on a planned effort. This corresponds with our commonsense experience.

If we look at the situation we are in as human beings here on earth, we will see that nothing can be created out of nothing. We can create, but all of our creative efforts must begin with an idea, a concept or a blueprint. If we try to create without a clearly defined blueprint, our creation either will not manifest or it will have an undesirable form.

Thus it is reasonable to conclude that the laws governing the evolution of the universe, without which everything would be chaos, are part of a plan. In order for such a plan to exist, there must be a mind or intelligence that has conceived of and formulated it. The problem is, where is this mind located? By going back to the idea that there could be spiritual octaves above and beyond the physical universe, we can find a home for this creative mind.

Our next question is why this creative mind decided to create us. Most of the phenomenon we observe in nature seem to be created for a specific purpose. The major difference between human beings and all other forms of life we know of is that our capacity of consciousness far exceeds that of any other living creature. Science has shown that most people use less than ten percent of their brain capacity to perform their daily functions of life. Might there be a reason why we have been given such a superior and seemingly unnecessary capacity of consciousness? We could imagine at least two purposes for our vast consciousness:

1. Having created an almost endless multitude of life forms, with an almost infinite variety, perhaps the creative mind decided to bring forth a life form with the capacity to understand and appreciate the intricacies of creation. Perhaps the mind wanted to create a being that could see beyond the outer, physical appearances of the universe and realize that they are only the effects of a hidden cause, namely the mind itself.

2. Is the reason for giving us this capacity of consciousness that we are meant to play an active role in the unfolding of the universe? Our vast consciousness could allow us to comprehend the laws under which the universe is evolving so that we could make active

use of these laws as co-creators. Perhaps we are part of the scheme and certain aspects of the blueprint cannot unfold without our conscious cooperation. Our consciousness could be one of the doors through which the blueprints from a higher world can be brought into physical manifestation.

The Issue of Free Will

If the creative mind wanted us to fully comprehend and appreciate the totality of life, it would have to give us a capacity of consciousness similar to its own—it created us in its own image and likeness. Because a creative mind must have total freedom to choose what and how to create, we must also be given this freedom of choice. Therefore, we are endowed with free will, which is another factor that sets us apart from other forms of life. Whereas all other life forms act upon instincts or patterns in their subconscious minds, a human being is not merely a piece of computer software. We have the capacity to make conscious choices.

By giving us free will, the creative mind must have been fully aware that there is the possibility for the misuse of freedom. You cannot give freedom without allowing for the misuse of freedom. When we are given the capacity to make choices, we are also given the capacity to make wrong choices.

At this point we must seek to define what we mean by wrong choices and it is quite simple. We are a part of a universe that is functioning according to universal laws and these laws serve to uphold the order and integrity of our world. These laws are set up to make sure that the evolution of the universe follows a balanced and harmonious path. As long as all forms of life act within the framework of the natural laws, their actions cannot be disruptive to the orderly progression of the universe. By giving us free will, it becomes possible that we can choose to ignore, disregard or willfully disobey natural laws. By so doing, we can disturb the harmony and balance of the universe, possibly with very destructive results. If we had the same power as the creative mind, one single individual could wreak havoc and possibly destroy the entire universe. Of course, this is not what the creator desires to see happen.

Therefore, we are given free will, but our full creative potential is not unlocked. In other words, we are given a limited potential to create and a limited potential to destroy.

If we follow this line of thought a little further, we could consider that earth is a schoolroom set up to give us a framework in which to exercise our creative faculties. We are here to get a "hands-on" education in how to be a co-creator. When we have learned to use the creative faculties we have here on earth, we might pass the final exam and go on to other levels of existence on which we have greater creative capacity—the spiritual octaves. But in order to pass the exam on earth, we must learn to use our faculties and our free will in a way that is not destructive to other parts of life—or, for that matter, to ourselves. When we have realized this principle, expressed in the Golden Rule and in the Buddhic principle of harmlessness, we can move on to greater responsibility. This is the concept expressed in the biblical quotation: "thou hast been faithful over a few things, I will make thee ruler over many things" *

At this point, we must take a little sidestep to deal with one of the popular misconceptions about free will. A good example of this is described in the book *People of the Lie*, by M. Scott Peck. He describes how a discussion with a client touches upon the subject of the purpose of life. The client has been taught the traditional Christian doctrine that we live for the glory of God. She rebels violently against this doctrine and expresses the belief that following God's will takes away her freedom of choice. It leaves no room for her and her will, individuality, or creativity.

This belief is very common and takes many subtle forms, but by comparing it to the thoughts expressed above, we can see that it is not correct. Living for the glory of God or following God's will is simply the religious person's way of saying that we live to help in the harmonious evolution of the universe. We live to be creative within the framework of natural laws. Seen from a larger perspective, which is not narrowly self-centered, this is not a restriction of our freedom or creativity. Following natural laws does not mean that we cannot be creative, express our individuality, or exercise our free will. Following natural laws is simply a matter of recognizing the mechanics of the situation we are in. It is much like driving a car. In order to make the car do what we want it to do for us,

* Matt. 25:23

we have to follow the laws of mechanics. If we are going 55 miles per hour on the highway and suddenly force the gear-shift in reverse, we are likely to damage the transmission. Then the car cannot take us to our desired destination. It simply does not make sense to say that because we cannot shift to reverse when we are going forward at 55 miles per hour the car is imposing a restriction on our free will and our individual creativity. This would be a self-centered and imma-ture way of reasoning.

Following the mechanics (timeless principles) of the situa-tion we are in is simply enlightened self-interest. Although it may cause us to make some temporary adjustments, it will enable us to reach our overall goal in the long run. Only a per-son who has no vision of a long-term goal for his or her exis-tence would see natural laws as a restriction of our freedom of choice. Unfortunately, many in our modern society are pro-grammed to have no such vision because they have been given no knowledge of their spiritual self.

It is simply not true that we can only choose freely by choosing to disobey natural laws. On the contrary, disobeying natural laws will inevitably cause harm to other forms of life. Saying that real freedom of choice can only be found through destructivity and disobedience is a lie. It may be a very persua-sive lie that the ego can disguise in many different, subtle forms, but it is still a lie. It may be one of the oldest lies found on this planet. It may even be the original lie with all other lies simply variations of this theme. If there is a force seeking to gain control over humankind, this is precisely the lie that could make it possible. As long as we are following the laws of na-ture, we will be protected by these laws and then we cannot be controlled by other people. The first step for someone who wants to gain control is to cause us to lose touch with natural law, and the way to do that is to make us misuse our free will. This is easily done by playing on the inherent tendencies of the human ego. The ego is very susceptible to the argument that the only true freedom is found by going beyond the "restric-tions" of natural law—"thou shalt not surely die" *. The viola-tion of natural law brings us to the subject of consequences.

* Gen. 3:44

Consequences

When the creative mind gave us free will, it must have known that eventually someone would use it in a way that was not in harmony with natural laws. Whether this is due to a willful disobedience of natural laws or an ignorance caused by an incomplete understanding, the results will be the same: inharmony and imbalance in the universe.

In order to bring the universe back into a state of balance, harmony must be reestablished and the disruptive influence neutralized. Who should do that? Well, what could be more logical than letting the person creating the inharmony do it? How can this be accomplished? What if there is a natural law that returns any inharmonious energy we send forth into the universe to us for balancing? One scientific parallel is Newton's law of action and reaction, but there may be another.

Modern science has taught us that the entire physical creation is an energy field. It is, therefore, not hard to imagine that all of our thoughts, feelings, or actions produce an energy impulse that spreads into the rest of the universe. Einstein speculated that if we traveled out into space and kept going in the same direction, we would return to our point of origin from the opposite direction, much like a planet following an orbit. Maybe all the energy we send out into the universe follows an orbit and then returns to us with the same qualification as we send it out: "whatsoever a man soweth, that shall he also reap." *

When we have violated natural laws and caused harm to other forms of life, we should be made aware of our error. In this way we can learn from mistakes and avoid repeating them, not because we fear punishment, but because we realize it is enlightened self-interest. The law described above would accomplish this, too. By returning all negatively qualified energy to the person sending it forth, this person is given a chance to realize what anyone with a credit card has been forced to learn: If you spend money today, it will reduce your ability to spend money tomorrow. By using our freedom of choice in violation of natural laws, we create inharmony in the universe. When this inharmonious energy comes back to us, it will restrict our ability to exercise our freedom; not because of

* Gal. 6:7

a judgmental God wanting to punish us, but because of the mechanics of our own wrong choices.

It follows that any actions that are in harmony with natural law would produce a positive influence in the universe and come back to us. This would have an expanding influence, giving us more freedom to act. Like investing money, it may cause some restriction in our ability to spend money today, but we will have greater freedom in the future.

At this point we must ask a very logical question. If the idea that all energy is returned to us is not part of our cultural and religious upbringing, how are we supposed to learn from it?

The reason I have given so much attention to the subjects of *free will*, *the mechanics of life* and *consequences* is that they explain why so many people in today's world have rejected orthodox religion. Many people feel a very deep-seated anger and resentment against what they have come to see as an unjust and judgmental God. This has caused them to have severe doubts about the spiritual aspects of life, some rejecting it entirely. I believe that through the understandings expressed earlier in this chapter, we can now resolve these feelings.

For many people one of the basic problems with orthodox religion is that it fails to explain some of the fundamental questions of life, such as why bad things happen to good people. How can we explain a person, who has followed the rules of both the church and state being suddenly faced with terminal illness, a crippling accident, rape, violence, or natural disaster? According to orthodox Christianity such misfortune is God's punishment for our sins. How can a person sin if he or she is following all the rules set by the church itself? And how can the concept of sin explain that some people are born with a crippling disease or under very unfortunate circumstances such as poverty or war? How can a newborn baby have sinned?

As we saw in Part Two, the early Church Fathers removed certain spiritual teachings from Christian doctrine. One of these teachings was the idea of the continuity of life; perhaps this idea could explain the questions raised above.

This teaching states that our real identity is the spiritual self or soul. This soul has a continued existence according to laws guiding a higher world. However, when the soul is inhabiting a physical body in this universe, it will be subject to at least some of the laws guiding the evolution of this world. One of these laws is the law of harmony or balance. If a soul misuses its free will and violates natural law, then it will, so to speak, create a debt to life. Since this debt is created in this universe, it must also be paid back here. What that means is that the soul cannot permanently leave this universe behind. If it has not balanced all debts when the physical body dies, then the soul is given a chance to come back into another body in order to balance the scales.

According to orthodoxy we only have one shot at salvation. If we have not atoned for our sins at the end of this life, we will, supposedly, burn in hell. This has created the image of a judgmental God, one who is watching our every thought and deed, ready to punish us harshly for even the slightest misconduct. Where did this image come from? I think historical fact shows us that from time to time, the orthodox Christian church has deliberately used fear to force the population into compliance with church doctrine. So, the forbidden question we might ask is: Does God want us to look upon him as a judgmental God, or was this image created for political reasons and thus another expression of the human ego?

Several modern theologians and psychologists have pointed out that the fear of a judgmental God is a very unhealthy mechanism that can give rise to a number of psychological problems. The most detailed description of this issue is found in the book *When God Becomes a Drug* by Father Leo Booth. Unfortunately, people who have exposed this problem have failed to come up with a more healthy image of God, but again the idea of continuity can provide it.

If the life we are living right now is not the first life, then it is obvious that our previous lives will have set the stage for our present one. Whatever misfortune we encounter, it could be the result of actions from past lives, things we did based on a freewill choice. What we experience as a misfortune is not God's punishment, it is an opportunity to balance our debts and give our soul greater spiritual freedom. It may be very difficult for us to go through the circumstances in this life, but it may free our soul in the long run. According to some of the near-death experiences, our souls will often choose to come into embodiment in a set of very difficult circumstances to more quickly balance a debt and be free to go on with life. What we see is that God is not trying to punish us through misfortune, there is simply a completely neutral natural law which returns all energy to us. If we see it as punishment, then we must say that we are really punishing ourselves. If we stick our finger in a light socket, the shock is not a punishment from the divine electrician, but a neutral effect of a natural law.

We realize that neither God nor natural law are respecters of persons, which is the only way to bring true justice into the universe. Throughout history, some people have sought to establish a society in which a small elite could do as it pleased. People with no respect for principles or natural laws could escape the consequences of their actions because they were protected by the system, the system acted like a buffer between them and natural law. This is widely recognized as injustice. The impersonal law described above makes sure that every erg of misqualified energy a person has sent forth is returned to us, regardless of our position in any man-made society. If it doesn't happen in the same lifetime, it will happen in a future life. A law returning all energy to its originator is perfect justice.

There are two basic ways to react to the idea of consequences. Principle-centered people will feel a sense of relief because they are happy to understand how a debt to life is created and how it can be paid back. Furthermore, it relieves them of all sense of guilt. Why feel guilty when you know it is possible to balance the scales and re-create the harmony of life? This leads to an entirely new relationship to the spiritual side of life in which all sense of doubt, fear and guilt is replaced by trust, joy and an enthusiastic drive to understand deeper layers of this exciting phenomenon called life.

As Scott Peck describes in his book, there is also a different reaction. Peck has found that some people completely refuse to consider that their actions could have any consequences. They refuse personal accountability and they refuse to change their views if it threatens their chosen beliefs. I think we can agree that this reaction is very typical for the human ego and its inherent need for self-justification. This might explain why our culture has no religious or spiritual teaching on consequences. It could have been deliberately removed by ego-centered people to justify their attempts to control the rest of us.

Evil as the Result of Choice

The idea of the continuity of life can do one more important thing for us. It can give us a new explanation of evil. According to an orthodox Christian perspective, it is difficult to explain evil. If all things are created by God, then evil is also created by God. Yet, this just doesn't make sense to most people. Why would God create something that willfully destroys his creation? In the Book of Revelation there is reference to angels rebelling against God's will and being cast out of heaven into the earth, but how this could possibly affect us today is inexplicable. Again, we end up with the standard phrase: It's a mystery. Furthermore, it makes evil seem like a preordained dilemma from which there is little hope of escape.

The deterministic scientific perspective is no better. The only way we might explain evil is as a polar opposite of good on a relative scale. It is a scientific assumption that the process of evolution has sustained life on this planet for billions of years. Why should this process suddenly produce something that is clearly self-destructive? Again, this seems very fatalistic with little hope for improving our situation. It doesn't explain why certain people are so radically evil.

How can there be a Hitler or Lenin? According to the Christian perspective, they, or their souls, must have been created by God like all other souls. Did God make a mistake or did he want them to be evil? According to the scientific perspective, they must be a product of hereditary or environmental factors. But Hitler's parents were not particularly evil. They were probably quite normal people. Many people have grown up under worse circumstances without becoming evil. How do we explain this?

If we take the idea of the continuity of life described above, we can present an explanation. Evil is not created by God, nor is it the result of heredity or environment. Since evil is not found in nature, only in people, we should consider what makes us different from other beings. The main difference is the ability to choose. What if we consider evil to be the consequence of choice, a wrong choice, a willful and deliberate disobedience of natural law? It does not have to be only one choice, it could be many choices made over many lifetimes. A specific lifestream could have rebelled against the laws of nature in so many lifetimes that a habit pattern has been created. When a soul exists independently of the physical body, it follows that the attributes of the soul, or at least some of them, can be carried from lifetime to lifetime. A person as evil as a Hitler did not suddenly pop up out of nowhere. The soul of such a person could have rebelled against natural law over many, many lifetimes and may now have reached a climax of rebellion. This could also explain why some evil people seem to be extremely powerful, having an ability to literally hypnotize others to follow them. They have had many lifetimes of practice.

Explaining evil as a result of choice immediately does away with all fatalistic ideas. With one swoop, we open up a new hope for the future of this planet. It would be a plausible explanation that much of the injustice throughout the centuries has been created by a limited number of lifestreams who will-fully rebel against natural law. Although these lifestreams may never choose to stop doing so, mankind at large could turn the situation around through choice.

In the Middle Ages, the population lived under one tyrannical ruler after another. Why? Because the people had not grown to an understanding of what was happening and how society could be changed. When this higher consciousness finally arrived, it forced a change and modern democracies appeared. Still, the same lifestreams may be among us today forming a power elite that is seeking to influence our society.

Today, they would seek to use the democratic principles to attain their goals, and as we shall examine later, this would be quite possible. Again, we can see that the population at large has not yet risen to a state of consciousness that can change this situation. Most people are not aware of how democracy is being misused to take away their freedom. Although they are generally frustrated and dissatisfied with the way things are going, they have not yet mustered the will to change it. We can see that if the majority of the population determines to look for a complete understanding of life and decides to look beyond the established doctrines to find it, a shift in consciousness can occur very quickly. Such a paradigm shift is always the first step in creating real progress in this world. The question is: Will people choose to look for such a new understanding, or will they choose to stay within the familiar framework in which they have been comfortable for so long?

CHAPTER 6

A New Human Right

Now let us consider what this new approach to life could tell us about abortion.

If we do have a spiritual self that has a continued existence beyond the physical body, then abortion is no longer a matter of aborting a life which we can choose to see as a person or a nonperson. It is a matter of aborting an opportunity, the opportunity for a soul to inhabit a physical body, and be a part of this material world for a time. Therefore, it makes no difference to the soul whether the abortion is performed in the ninth month, the second month or on the second day. At any point after conception, an abortion will take away the soul's opportunity. In fact, to the soul it will make no difference if this happens through an abortion or by killing the baby after it is born; the opportunity is lost either way.

Some people might ask, "So, what is the big deal if a soul loses an opportunity to be in embodiment, if that life would have been filled with poverty and misery?" As we have seen above, even if a person's life is less than ideal according to a materialistic standard, the soul of this person could still be experiencing a spiritual growth. Even the most difficult circumstance could be chosen by the soul for the purpose of a more rapid growth. How can we judge the spiritual purpose behind another person's situation? How can we say that certain souls should not be given a chance to live?

If we accept that the basic purpose of life is spiritual

growth, then we can conclude that there is a crying need to re-define our ideas of human rights. The concept of the right to "Life, liberty and the pursuit of happiness" has served us well, but it is now time to ascend to a higher understanding of these rights. We can therefore define a new right, which is the most fundamental right yet discovered—the right to spiritual growth, the right to grow!

If this right was accepted and incorporated into our philo-sophical basis, it would lead to a complete and all-pervading adjustment of every aspect of society. All other rights would spring from this one right. All laws would be defined by evaluating whether an act would enhance or destroy the oppor-tunity for spiritual growth. Suddenly we would have a new definition of crime, since the worst possible crime would be to destroy the opportunity for spiritual growth, be it for oneself or for others. Right now our society is heavily influenced by the human ego and its trivial need to justify its existence and short-term desires. By acknowledging the right to grow, we could begin to create a new type of society in which the main goal is to give the greatest possible number of souls the oppor-tunity for spiritual growth that this planet has to offer.

Therefore, the central question in the abortion debate really should be: How does an abortion affect the spiritual growth of the souls of the unborn child, the mother, the father and every-one else involved?

The Abortion of a Soul

If an abortion takes away the opportunity of a soul, then we must consider how this could affect the soul. It will deny the soul an ability to learn, to express its individuality and to pay back its debts to life. If life is a continuum, then the soul could be affected for a long time into the future by missing an oppor-tunity to be in embodiment. A specific soul could have an important contribution to make in the world at a certain time. If such a soul is aborted, it might be impossible for it to give the same contribution at another time since society will have moved on. A soul may never get another chance to enter the world under the exact same circumstances.

We could consider that a soul had to reembody at a certain time and in a certain set of circumstances to balance a specific debt to life. By being aborted, the soul will miss this opportunity, and it could become harder to pay off the debt in the future. Even cases of incest and rape could be the result of past actions (by the child or parents), and one way a soul must enter the world to pay back its specific debt to life.

We might consider if there could be a tie between certain souls, if they have been together in past lifetimes. They could have a mission to fulfill together or they have created a debt to each other that they have to balance by being together in this lifetime. This could explain why we sometimes meet a stranger and feel we know him or her. We may have been friends in the past life. It would also explain why we sometimes feel an intense dislike for a stranger, that person might have harmed us in a prior lifetime.

What if an abortion is not only a loss to the soul aborted but also to the potential parents? The parents might have a mission to fulfill in life that requires the help of one or more of their children. Maybe the parents have a debt to pay back to one or more lifestreams, and they have been given an opportunity to give birth to these lifestreams. The potential parents may be missing an important opportunity for soul growth by having an abortion.

Some of the questions outlined above could possibly be illumined by the books *Life Between Life* (mentioned earlier) and *Life Before Life*, by Helen Wambach. These books describe how professional psychologists used hypnosis to regress a great number of people back to the time before their birth. Hypnotic regression has been widely used by psychologists over the past two decades and although it may not be a mainstream practice, it is widely accepted. It is interesting that many of the things people experienced during hypnosis correspond to the near-death experiences.

Many of the subjects recalled being on a higher level of reality, often with spiritual counselors and their parents-to-be. Often they knew why they had to embody in that particular circumstance and it was the soul's freewill choice to embody, even under less than ideal conditions. If we accept that our conscious awareness is only the tip of the iceberg of our consciousness, we realize that many of the conditions we are facing today could be the result of choices made by our soul for a long-term purpose. It may be hard for us to face circumstances right now when we have no conscious awareness of our soul's choices. When we consider that our present hardships could be the means to future freedom, it becomes easier to bear almost any circumstance. How many young women would choose not to have an abortion if they had this perspective and accepted the truth of it in their own hearts?

In many cases, the decision to have an abortion is the result of a "here and now choice." The woman is in a more or less desperate state of consciousness, and one of the characteristics of stress or emotional pressure is that it makes it impossible for people to think ahead. Anyone who has studied the techniques used by propaganda experts will know that the basis for all propaganda is to temporarily shut off people's ability to think ahead, to envision a long span of time. The shorter the time span people are able to consider, the more they can be manipulated.

Having to face the dilemma of an unplanned pregnancy catapults many women into emotional distress, making it very difficult for them to consider their long-term interests. If we are truly concerned about helping these women, we must make sure that they do not make a decision they will regret later. The only way to do that is to help them to look beyond their present situation and gain a long-term perspective on life. The idea of life as a continuum could be one way of providing such a perspective.

Another perspective is the view that the soul might not be entirely feminine or masculine. In other words, in some lives the soul might embody in a female body and in others in a male body. This perspective would shed new light on one of the very powerful forces in the abortion debate: women's liberation and liberation of the sexes. Perhaps a woman is more than a woman. Perhaps she is an immortal soul which, in this specific lifetime, has taken on a female body? Could the reason for this be that the soul needs to be in a female body to learn and grow spiritually? Perhaps it needs to pay back a debt to life, which can only be accomplished in a woman's body, such as bearing children? Or the soul voluntarily chose to embody in a female body before this life because it knew that this would give the best opportunity for growth?

It could be the result of an incomplete understanding that some women, in the name of equal rights, refuse to follow the mechanics of being a woman. Could they in reality be refusing to follow their spiritual calling and ignoring the choice of their own soul? Maybe having children really isn't a limitation for a woman, but the means to her soul's long-term liberation?

How Does It Feel to Be Aborted

The perspective that we could have a soul consciousness before our birth forces us to consider that the unborn baby could be conscious in the womb. Does a soul have a conscious experience of an abortion? If so, how does it feel? Is there physical pain? There must be emotional pain when a life, an opportunity, is cut off before it even begins. Does the soul end up having emotional scars that may linger in the subconscious even when the soul comes into embodiment again?

One of the consequences of Einstein's contribution to physics is that we must consider the entire universe to be an energy field. All matter is simply a form of energy. In the universe there is a constant interaction between different forms of energy, whether we see it or not. What happens on an energy level when a soul (which is an energy field) gets attached to a fetus in the womb? Does it happen all at once, or is it a gradual process of integration that lasts the entire nine months and is only completed just before birth (or even continues after birth)? If it is a gradual process, then what happens when a fetus is aborted and the integration process comes to a halt? How does the soul get disentangled from the dead fetus and how does it affect the soul?

Since the mother is also an energy field, what happens to her in the process of pregnancy? The fetus is created from the body of the mother. It seems logical to assume that some of her energy, her life-force, is involved in the formation of the fetus. What happens to the mother's energy field when an abortion occurs? Is she affected on a subconscious level, does she lose some of her life-force? Is this the real reason for the so-called Post Abortion Syndrome (PAS) which a number of women go through after an abortion? Recent studies done by a pro-choice group have shown that as many as 90 percent of all women experience PAS. If the woman's energy field is damaged by an abortion, is it any wonder she can experience severe emotional problems afterwards? Is it any wonder it can take many years to heal this emotional wound?

It is interesting to see how we fail to apply the discoveries of modern science to the fundamental questions of life. Since Einstein formulated his theory of relativity, we have had the perspective that life is an interchange of energy. Energy can appear as matter, but it can also appear in a form that cannot be detected by our physical senses or traditional scientific methods. No complete understanding of life can ever be gained by looking at life from the perspective of matter alone. Life has two sides, a physical and a nonphysical or spiritual. To know the totality of life we must look at both sides of the coin.

One aspect of being a co-creator is obviously the bringing forth of children. Since the creative mind has manifested the universe out of itself, it must be present in every part of the universe and it must be seeking to express itself through all life. Thus, it is also present in the child, even the unborn child, and in a way, it could be said that abortion is the abortion of the creator itself.

Consequences, Again

To be completely honest, we must also consider consequences. If having an abortion is causing harm to oneself or another soul, we can conclude that it is creating imbalance and inharmony in the universe. If so, then it must be a violation of natural laws and it follows that there must be a price to pay. The people deciding to have an abortion must incur a debt to life, which will have to be balanced sometime in the future. Maybe this will limit their freedom, and maybe they would not have chosen to have the abortion if they had been aware of these consequences.

How can we claim that abortion should be a matter of individual choice, when the individual is not fully aware of the consequences of that choice? When someone is telling a woman that having an abortion is a matter of her private choice and that it will have no consequences whatsoever for herself or anyone else, are they promoting a very limited and potentially wrong attitude to life? Are they tempting the woman into limiting her own future freedom, placing her in a situation she would not have chosen had she known the full impact of her choice?

Assuming that nothing in life comes free and that all our actions have consequences, we conclude abortion must have consequences. Saying it has no consequences could very well cause people to limit, unknowingly, their long-term freedom. Ironically, this is done in the name of freedom of choice. What is true freedom òf choice? If there is any spiritual reality to life, it follows that each of our choices must have consequences. This is confirmed by science in the law of cause and effect. If we do not know the consequences, how can we evaluate if the price we have to pay in the long-run is worth the temporary benefit of our choice? How can we ever separate choice from the consideration of the consequences? An active attempt to make people do so could be a subtle form of manipulation.

CHAPTER 7

The Question of Guilt

Our discussion of abortion would not be complete without touching upon the subject of guilt. Guilt is another hidden player in the debate that the idea of the continuity of life can give us a new perspective on.

For quite some time, some people have been very direct in calling an abortion "murder." The logical consequence is that most of the women who ever had an abortion must be considered murderers. Most of the men having influenced the women's decisions would be accomplices to murder. Actually, everyone who has ever supported abortion would be partly to blame for the murder of 25 million unborn babies. This means that as many as 30 to 50 million people, almost 20 percent of the nation's population, have been directly involved with murder. A larger percentage of the population has to some degree been supportive of this murder (that is, tax supported abortions). The anti-abortion people may not have said this directly, but it has surely been said between the lines.

There is no question that such a viewpoint will cause an emotional reaction among the people belonging to the target group. It is safe to say that very few people will be completely untouched by the accusation that they could be guilty of, or involved with, murder. There is a wide range of possible emotional reactions to such an accusation, but let us stay with the basic idea of this book. We started out by saying that if there is to be a true resolution to the abortion controversy, we will

have to look beyond our paradigms. How will the proclama-
tion that abortion is murder affect people's ability or willingness to change their position?

The answer to this question will depend largely on the individual and his or her ability to handle the feeling of guilt. If
accused of being involved with murder, most people will inevitably feel a spark of guilt, whether they are consciously
aware of it or not. The sense of guilt or remorse is a feeling
that, for most people, is quite uncomfortable. They could easily do without it and, as we shall see later, they probably
should do without it. For now, let us state that a great number
of people will go to great lengths to avoid feeling guilty for
their actions or their viewpoints. The two most common ways
we seek to avoid a sense of guilt are withdrawal and self-
justification. All of us have both of these tendencies latent in
our psychology because they are characteristics of the ego.

When people are exposed to a situation that causes a violent emotional reaction they are not able to handle in a balanced
way, they often respond with withdrawal. In the case of the
abortion issue, they might react by trying to shut the issue out
of their consciousness. They refuse to consider the issue or to
formulate, much less express, an opinion about it. To them it
becomes a taboo subject they refuse to deal with because dealing with it represents a danger. The danger could be very real
since dealing with the issue could stir up a violent emotional
reaction causing severe psychological problems. This type of
reaction is quite common among women who have had an
abortion, a problem largely ignored in the debate.

Neither of the two sides in the debate have been willing to
come up with much support for people with this problem and
the reason is simple. To some pro-life proponents these people
are either murderers or sinners or both. The only way they can
help these people is by offering them a way out of the sense of
guilt, which could weaken their case that abortion is unconditionally wrong. To some pro-choice proponents, any sense of
guilt over an abortion is completely unnecessary, even imma-
ture. They could only help by acknowledging that feelings of
remorse could be justified, which would weaken their case that
abortion is unconditionally acceptable. Both sides in the debate
are caught by their respective doctrines and by their chosen
approach to the debate.

People in a psychological dilemma concerning abortion are
caught in the middle with no place to go. If they were to

acknowledge that abortion is wrong, they would have to admit that they had committed murder, and this they are not capable of doing. Their only way out seems to be complete emotional withdrawal from the issue. Neither the pro-life nor the pro-choice approaches are going to help these people change their position on the issue.

Another form of withdrawal is to focus all of the attention on one particular viewpoint. An example is the idea that since the fetus is not yet a person, abortion is not murder. Some people concentrate on this one point, using it to maintain their sense of equilibrium. They feel that because of this one piece of argumentation, they do not have to change or reconsider their position. If they hear conflicting viewpoints, they will immediately dismiss them as untrue or irrelevant. Or, they may simply shut them out of their consciousness and refuse to consider them. The statement that abortion is murder only makes it harder for these persons to change or even reconsider their position on the issue.

Self-justification

When pro-life proponents openly declare that abortion is murder, it is immediately predictable that some people will engage in an attempt to refute this declaration to justify their own position. In fact, most of the people who are supportive of abortion are likely to do this since they would not be able to live with the accusation. Murder is a strong accusation that very few people are able to live with unresolved.

It is easy to see that the pro-choice movement is to some degree affected by this need for self-justification. Some of the arguments presented by this movement are highly intellectual (i.e., the fetus is human life, but it is not a person, thus it is not protected by the Constitution, and thus abortion is not murder). They are directed towards justifying the act of abortion and the existence of the pro-choice movement.

When people go into a state of consciousness in which they are driven by a need or desire for self-justification, it becomes extremely difficult for them to change or reconsider their position. They will most likely take one of two routes:

1. They will focus their attention on one or several points of argumentation that for them seems to justify their position. They will then withdraw from the issue, refusing to consider any conflicting viewpoints. They have created a framework in which they are comfortable and they don't want to look beyond it.

2. They will actively seek to convert other people to their viewpoint, seeking to influence society to get their position acknowledged by a governmental authority. Many people feel that since the U. S. Supreme Court legalized abortion in 1973, the question of whether abortion is right or wrong has become obsolete. For them, it is no longer a question of considering whether abortion is right or wrong according to some higher truth, but a matter of defending the right to have an abortion from those who are seeking to terminate it. These people have let the Supreme Court do their thinking for them—or perhaps they believe the Supreme Court can decide what is truth regardless of higher principles.

To understand fully the effects of the consciousness of self-justification, we must consider that it tends to block the acceptance of eternal values or a higher truth. For a person seeking to justify his actions or viewpoints, it is often undesirable to consider the existence of a higher truth or of timeless values. In most cases, it becomes easier to look for tendencies in the time we live in that will justify the chosen position. We have to consider that the need for self-justification will almost automatically turn a person into either a relativist or humanist. This is not a political judgment but a matter of observing one of the tendencies in human psychology. When we are in a defensive state of mind, we tend to look for a way out. In our eagerness to escape the uncomfortable feeling of guilt (and the self-condemnation that goes with it), we often "forget" about eternal values since relative values offer us a more convenient way out.

This observation prompts us to ask why the pro-life proponents are using the argument that abortion is murder? With a basic understanding of human psychology, it is easy to see that such an argument is not likely to produce the desired results, rather it will cause people to become defensive. If the pro-life people truly want to save the lives of the unborn, why would they use an argument that can only have the contrary effect?

We can find the answer by looking at the roots of the pro-life movement. We have observed that the pro-life movement is influenced by orthodox Christian doctrine. We have also noted that modern Christian churches have not gone back in time. They have not uprooted the deliberate errors or unintended misconceptions that earlier church leaders incorporated into the Christian faith. If we look at the Dark Ages, we see that the Christian church was an extremely powerful political factor in the feudal societies of Europe. Whereas the king had an army and weapons to enforce his powers, the church ruled by an invisible power, the combination of guilt and fear. Through the doctrine of original sin, people were programmed to believe that they were sinners by their very existence. They were brought up to fear the consequences of their sins and to believe that the only way out was blind obedience to church doctrine. Thus, the earlier Christian churches deliberately ruled through guilt and fear.

The declaration that abortion is murder could be a modern version of this attempt to rule through guilt and fear. There seems to be no other reason for using this argument. Is it an attempt to make people reverse their viewpoints on abortion by making them feel guilty and fear the consequences? In our modern times such an attempt is doomed from the very beginning. Using guilt and fear will only affect those people who believe in the traditional Christian doctrine and they are most likely already against abortion.

On the other hand, for anyone who believes in the modern scientific doctrine, guilt has no constructive effect. They see it as another attempt from the Christians to beat them into submission with hellfire and brimstone and they inevitably go into a defensive state of consciousness. The orthodox Christians are simply caught by their traditional approach and they cannot free themselves from it. The non-Christians are also caught by their own paradigms. In their eagerness to defend themselves against the Christian accusations, they refuse to consider spiritual perspectives.

What we see is that the battle between these two approaches causes us to lose sight of the one element that could bring a true resolution to the abortion controversy. In the battle between man-made doctrines, we forget to look for guiding principles that are not man-made but reach beyond our own little world. Could this be the real problem in the abortion debate?

Positive Versus Negative Motivation

Today, many people see Christianity, possibly all religion, as an attempt to control people and their actions. If we go back to the beginning and take a look at Jesus and his methods, we must admit that he was not a hellfire and brimstone preacher. Jesus did not seek to use fear and guilt to make people change their actions—he sought to set people free from guilt and fear. By his direct example and teachings he, as all other true religious leaders, sought to give people a higher understanding of the reality of life. He wanted people to change their ways and sought to accomplish this through positive motivation. He knew if he could get people to accept a higher understanding of life, their actions would automatically change in enlightened self-interest. He sought to give people a positive motivation for freeing themselves from the bonds of the ego and instead centering themselves in principles.

This brings us back to the concept that we must choose between being ego-centered or principle-centered. For principle-centered people it can be said that if they knew better, they would do better. Not so with ego-centered people. They would not do better if they knew better, but in most cases they will never get to know better. Their egos will come up with a perfect excuse for why they don't have to reconsider their opinions. Ego-centered people are not open to a higher understanding of life. They want to stay where they are comfortable, and they want all other people to confirm their position. They don't want to have a society that is based on an understanding of natural law and a higher truth.

Let us go back to the idea that it is enlightened self-interest to have our personal lives and our society based on natural law. True religion is handed down to us from a higher source for three reasons: (1) to give us a higher understanding of the mechanics of our situation—natural law; (2) to give us a set of outer guidelines that will prevent us from violating natural law until our understanding has grown to where we can see natural law directly; and (3) to give us the means to atone for our wrong choices and pay back the debt to life incurred through our violation of natural law.

Religion is meant to give us the means to graduate from earth's schoolroom and thereby set us free to ascend to higher levels of learning. Since our free will is the ultimate factor influencing whether we will graduate or not, religion can only work for us if we accept it through a freewill choice. Such a choice must be based on an understanding of why the principles of that particular religion represent enlightened self-interest. If this understanding is missing, what is left?—Only an outer shell of doctrine and rules which many people see as a restriction of free will. When the spiritual understanding is lost, only outer doctrine is left, and this doctrine cannot give people the positive motivation they need.

If we take the idea that the formation of the Christian church was to some extent affected by ego-centered people, they could have, either willfully or unknowingly, caused the loss of at least part of the spiritual understanding given to us through Jesus. As this disappeared, leaving only an outer doctrine, many people lost the positive motivation for accepting the Christian faith. Over the centuries, it became increasingly difficult for the Church to make people accept the Christian faith through a positive motivation. This could explain why the Church, up through the Middle Ages, became increasingly rigid and enforced blind acceptance to outer doctrine. It could explain why guilt and fear gradually assumed a more prominent role as the means to make people accept doctrine. When the Church was no longer able to provide the positive motivation, the leaders had to find other means to stay in power. They sought to induce a sense of guilt and fear to force people to accept their version of the Christian faith. They sought to force people into submission and to set themselves, the rulers of church hierarchy, up as the saviors. Again the problem is the ego-centered people themselves. In their inability or unwillingness to accept the living understanding of reality given through Jesus, they cause the formation of a dead outer doctrine. They then seek to force people into accepting this doctrine as the only means to salvation. Guilt and fear have now replaced understanding as the motivating factor.

As mentioned earlier, the loss of the original understanding caused many people to lose faith in Christianity and as a counterreaction the modern scientific doctrine was formed. What we have to understand is that the mechanistic science is a product of the same state of consciousness that created the rigid Christian doctrine. We have not been liberated from the errors of doctrinal Christianity; we have merely been propelled into the other extreme.

Let us stay with guilt. The medieval churches, including the Protestant churches since they did not go back to the source and remove the errors of the Catholic church, merely built on the foundation set by the early Catholic church fathers. They created a very rigid and restrictive approach a "nothing goes" attitude. This caused a counterreaction, and as a result, a new philosophy emerged that took us into the opposite extreme. Modern intellectual doctrine states that there is no absolute truth, therefore nothing is really wrong and anything goes. The Christians say we have to feel guilty for just being alive and the humanists say we don't have to feel guilty for anything.

We must understand that there could be a golden middle way between these two extremes. The key is to realize that the two extremes are both a product of the same kind of consciousness, which is a denial of the responsibility to discriminate.

The Christian church started out with a true foundation, a set of principles handed down to us from a higher source, therefore representing a higher truth. Over the centuries, this original delivery was distorted and ideas were added unto it—the product of the human ego. Most people with a rudimentary knowledge of church history realize that certain church leaders added and subtracted ideas to the original Christian message according to the political situation of their times. What happened was that the higher truth became mixed with ego-centered ideas. Since church leaders could not and would not admit this, they had to enforce this mixed doctrine as if it was the pure truth. They could not do this by giving people a higher understanding because no such understanding existed for the man-made elements, so they had to do it by seeking to force people to follow the rules without asking questions. What happened in this process was that the church, its leaders and members, stopped asking the most basic question we humans must ask: Is this a principle-centered or an ego-centered idea? The Church no longer sought to discriminate between the two, and the very idea that there was a need to discriminate had been replaced by church doctrine.

The modern scientific, or intellectual humanist approach

was born as a reaction against this rote, outer doctrine. It states that there are many religions, each of them claiming to represent the only true God and have the only truth. Since they obviously cannot all be right, it is logical that there is no such thing as a higher truth and that all religion is just a product of man's mind. According to this reasoning, it is perfectly natural for us to define our own reality and we should not even look for such an elusive and illusory thing as a "higher truth." As a result of the idea that there is no higher truth, there can be nothing that is really "wrong"—anything goes and we can do whatever we want without feeling guilty about it. Although this approach seems to be diametrically opposite the doctrinal approach, it really isn't. It springs from the same state of consciousness.

Neither the old doctrinal approach, nor the modern approach, is seeking to discriminate between principles handed down from a higher source and ideas springing from human minds. They are both the results of a complete denial of the responsibility to discriminate. The ultimate triumph of the human ego is the belief that we do not have to discriminate between human and principle-centered ideas.

This is the tragedy of our modern times and the present abortion debate. In our striving to escape one form of tyranny, we have propelled ourselves, or allowed the ego-centered people to propel us, into another form of the same tyranny. True freedom can only be found if both the individual life and the life of society are based on ideas that are not defined by human minds. The basis for this freedom is the ability to discriminate between what is a higher truth and what is a man-made "truth." If the willingness and ability to make this discrimination has been aborted, the only question left is which one of the many tyrants will be ruling our lives!

No Black and White Judgments

I want to make it very clear that I am not trying to say that the pro-life position is principle-centered and the pro-choice position is ego-centered. When evaluating the abortion issue, we must realize that it is impossible to make a simple black and white judgment. We must admit that it is quite possible to hold either position from an ego-centered state of mind. Let us look at a couple of examples. Say we have a person who believes that, according to his religion, abortion is a sin that must be stopped. This person has two options, he can seek to make people agree with his position by expanding their understanding, or he can seek to force them into compliance. A principle-centered person would seek to formulate a body of spiritual teachings that would give people a deeper understanding of life so they would be motivated to stop abortion. If he could not find such a teaching in his own religious doctrine, he would look beyond it. He might even do this to reach people with different religious convictions. A principle-centered person would have no need to convert everybody else to one particular faith. He would simply seek to provide a higher understanding of life so people could have a better foundation for their personal choices.

An ego-centered person would be firmly convinced that his belief is the only true one and that all others should be made to follow it. He could seek to accomplish this in three ways. He could try to convert everyone else' to his religion. He could seek to scare them with hellfire, brimstone and eternal damnation. He could work to mount a political pressure causing the government to stop abortion by law. This approach is geared towards forcing a compliance in the outer world instead of producing an inner, spiritually based acceptance. We could say that a pro-life person who is willing to force others, but unwilling to give them a higher spiritual understanding, is in all reality reacting in an ego-centered way.

As another example, we could look at a person who believes abortion should be a matter of individual choice. This person has the same two options; he can work for a higher understanding or for an outer compliance. If a person says that a woman has a right to choose even though she has no understanding of the potential effects of her choice, then this position is ego-centered. He is clearly ignoring the possibility that a woman could limit her future opportunities for growth and he has no desire to expand her spiritual understanding. On the other hand, a pro-choice person might say that since our society, so far, has been unable to come up with a teaching on the (spiritual) consequences of abortion, we have no right to say that a woman cannot make that choice. If we are not seeking to give her an understanding of the consequences of her choice, we should not tell her how to choose. To this we must agree. It would not be according to our democratic foundation to prohibit smoking without giving people an understanding of how it affects their health. We can therefore say, that such a position would be principle-centered, as long as the person was simultaneously working to bring forth a spiritual teaching that would give us a higher understanding of the issue. He would also have to be willing to change his position on the issue, if this new understanding called for it.

Accountability Without Guilt

Let us find a golden middle way between the excessively restrictive and the overly permissive approaches. A starting point could be the idea that life is a cosmic learning process in which we grow in understanding of natural law. It seems logical to assume that there are different levels of this understanding and therefore different levels of responsibility. It would not be right to expect a kindergarten student to perform geometry, and there is no reason why he should feel guilty for not being able to do so. It has been said that to enter heaven we must become as little children. The main characteristic of a child is that he or she approaches life with an innocent attitude, an open mind. If a child is trying to walk and falls down, it immediately gets up and tries again. It does not consider that it has made a mistake and does not feel guilty for not being perfect. The child does not go into a defensive attitude or reason that it didn't really want to learn how to walk. What is the big deal about walking anyway? The child does not allow any of these feelings to hold it back, it simply keeps trying until it has attained mastery.

As we grow older, the elements of guilt, shame, doubt and fear enter our consciousness and we begin to allow them to hold us back. Negative feelings often prevent us from trying again because we feel self-condemnation for not being perfect. We have begun to pass a value judgment on ourselves according to a standard passed onto us from without. Many people allow this standard to affect most of their thoughts, feelings and actions; yet, they never question the standard itself. It is like seeing everything through colored glasses without ever considering if the glasses have the right color or if we need any glasses in the first place. We need to consider if this judgmental standard comes from a higher source or if it originated from human minds.

There is no cosmic necessity forcing God to give man free will. He could just as easily have created man as a kind of robot, an intelligent animal that could only follow certain instincts. By giving man free will, God must have known it was possible we would choose to go against natural law. He must have known that through repetition of such choices we could gradually lose our understanding for natural law. This could create a downward spiral that could cause humankind to "fall" into a lower state of consciousness, a state in which we lose the direct contact with God and clear understanding of natural law—perhaps even all memory of the spiritual world.

He must have known that it would be possible for us to fall to the point of believing everything to be relative because we had lost all contact with His higher reality. It is not likely that God wanted us to fall into this low state of consciousness, however, he respects our free will and allowed it to happen. Since this limited state of consciousness is the cause of all the misery and evil we find on this planet, God probably wants us to get out of it, the sooner the better. But He does not want to force us out of it. He wants us to come out of it through a conscious, freewill choice in which we accept a higher level of consciousness in enlightened self-interest.

If this is so, then God would want to make it as easy as possible for us to make that choice. He would not want to put anything upon us that would cause us to hold ourselves back and prevent us from accepting a higher understanding. It is not likely that God would put feelings of doubt, guilt and fear of consequences upon us. He would not want us to condemn ourselves, He would not want society to condemn us and He would not condemn us for our mistakes. As long as we are in a limited state of consciousness in which we do not have the full understanding of natural law, it is unavoidable that we make mistakes. God does not want us to dwell on our mistakes. He wants us to learn from them, so we can use them as a stepping stone for attaining a higher understanding in which we no longer make mistakes.

Some people who have gone through near-death experiences have described how they were taken to a higher level of reality and shown every moment of their lives as if on a screen playing before their eyes. Their mistakes were pointed out to them, but in a nonjudgmental way, without any trace of condemnation. These people were greatly comforted by their experience and felt reborn because they were set free from the heavy burden of guilt, fear and condemnation which society has programmed into our subconscious minds for centuries. These people had a greater understanding of the wrong their actions had done to others and of their free choice to do better.

For people in a predominantly principle-centered state of consciousness, those who would do better if they knew better, there is no constructive purpose for allowing the feeling of guilt. It can only serve to hold them back in their spiritual growth, and this is neither in their own best interest, nor in the interest of life itself. Therefore, we can conclude that doubt, fear, guilt and self-condemnation are altogether negative feelings that do not serve any positive purpose. They are not of God, but a product of the human ego. They do not help us grow, but serve to hold us back, which then allows ego-centered people to gain power over us.

Let us transfer this perspective to the abortion debate. We have seen that an abortion denies the soul an opportunity to be in embodiment. It prevents the soul from learning and paying back its debts to life, and causes it to miss an important opportunity for spiritual progress. Therefore, we see that, according to a higher understanding of reality, abortion is not in harmony with natural law. It creates inharmony and imbalance in the universe. Saying that abortion is wrong does not mean that we have to feel guilty about it. If a woman has had an abortion, her decision was a product of the understanding she had at the time. Her understanding may have been limited; it may even have been influenced by other people with a limited understanding. She did not intentionally do something wrong, and it does not make sense to say that she committed murder. She made the best possible choice with the level of understanding she had at the time. Since she is a person with a love for life, it is natural for her to strive to expand her understanding of life. If this higher understanding causes her to realize that her former actions were not in her own best interest, she does not need to feel guilty about it. She should not allow the negative feeling of guilt to prevent her from accepting and following her new and higher understanding. By accepting the new understanding, by correcting her former attitude and by deciding to change her actions accordingly, she is "blameless before the Lord." She should simply learn from her past mistakes and use them constructively to come up higher in consciousness.

Since her past choice has created an imbalance in the universe, the woman who has chosen to have an abortion has incurred a debt to life. The fact that she should not feel guilt does not mean that she should abandon all responsibility for her past actions. On the contrary, by avoiding guilt, it becomes possible for her to accept full accountability for her actions. Instead of withdrawing or seeking self-justification, she can approach the situation with an objective, nondefensive attitude. She can calmly accept that she has incurred a debt to life and that she will have to repay it to restore balance and harmony. She will not see this as a punishment but as a way to attain higher personal freedom.

The means to pay back the debt to life caused by an abortion could be many. Every major religion describes a set of general ways to balance the scales and pay back our debts. In the Christian tradition, they are: prayer, fasting, penance, good works or service to others. In the case of abortion, we could mention several specific ways:

1. Have another child. Even if this does not completely alter the first abortion, it gives another soul an opportunity for growth.

2. If this is not possible, adopt a child that might otherwise have been aborted.

3. Work to expand other people's understanding by telling them about the personal transformation. Nothing helps people more than hearing the story of how another person like themselves has grown to a higher understanding.

4. Work to make it easier for a pregnant woman to choose adoption rather than abortion.

These actions could also be applicable for people who have performed abortions, people who have caused others to have an abortion or people who have been involved with the pro-abortion efforts. In other words, there is a way out for everybody. By adopting a positive attitude and allowing oneself to accept a higher understanding of life, we can gain a new perspective on feelings of guilt and self-condemnation. Instead of continuing to hold ourselves back in a limited state of consciousness, we can win a new sense of soul freedom.

A True Resolution
to the Controversy?

If a large number of people dared look beyond the paradigms and doctrines they have been brought up to accept, if they dared to explore and develop the intuitive faculties anchored in their own hearts, and if they, by so doing, found something that could be described somewhat like the approach to life we have outlined above, it could resolve the conflict over abortion overnight. The discussion of what society should do about abortion would become completely obsolete, by bringing the decision down to the level where it really belongs in a democratic society—the individual human being.

Here is another way in which the abortion debate has been off track. So far, all the attention has been on how society should deal with abortion. What should the legislators, the politicians, the lawmakers do about it? Far too much attention has been given to what a handful of people—the presiding Supreme Court judges—should do about abortion. It is as if they were the ones running our "democracy"—they are not, or at least they shouldn't be. "We, the people" should be running our democratic society. The ideal outcome of the conflict over abortion would be that "we, the people" would stand united because, by looking honestly into our individual hearts, we have gained a higher understanding—not only a higher understanding of abortion, but of life itself. This new understanding can tell us how to bring our society in touch with the principles governing the evolution of life in the universe. It will also tell us how we can make the best use of the mechanics of our situation instead of blindly seeking to force the gearshift into reverse while going 55 miles per hour down the highway of life while complaining that life is not what we want it to be.

To Grow or Not to Grow?

The inescapable reality of life in this physical world is that we can never escape making choices. All of our actions, even our lack of actions, represent choices. Ultimately, every choice we make is a question of whether we choose life and growth, or stagnation and death. The choice we are facing in all of life's various situations is whether to respond in a principle- or ego-centered way.

When we have accepted that life has a spiritual side, we can redefine these concepts. Since the essence of life is growth, especially spiritual growth, we can see that a principle-centered person will always choose to grow. He or she is choosing to seek greater understanding of all aspects of the situation. Gaining greater understanding of the physical world is also a part of spiritual growth.

An ego-centered person will ignore or deny the spiritual side of life and the need for growth. Such a person will stagnate and gradually lose touch with the principles, natural laws, governing life. The soul of such a person will not have its inherent drive for growth fulfilled and this will create a feeling of emptiness. This lack will have to be covered over by some of the many means available in our modern society (i.e., power, material possessions, drugs, alcohol, sex).

The important thing to understand is that most of us have both tendencies latent in our psychology. We are responding in a principle-centered way most of the time, but certain factors will trigger an ego-centered reaction. Two of the most common factors that force us into an ego-centered reaction are physical and mental fatigue. When we become tired, we lose the ability to think ahead and we focus on our immediate situation. Other factors creating this effect are the negative emotions of fear, doubt or anger. When we feel anger towards another person, we lose the ability or willingness to work for that person's spiritual growth. This, in turn, causes us to limit our own spiritual growth, which we often fail to see. An ego-centered reaction can be a one-time affair, but quite often it gains a more permanent character because it creates a need for self-justification, which causes us to look for reasons to feel angry. We look for faults in others and even the slightest imperfection will be used to build our case. Hereby, anger towards another person will become permanent and that forces us into an ego-centered reaction every time we meet that person or perhaps even when we think about him or her. This can lead to a state of mind in which we become consumed by anger or hatred to the point where these, in reality, very self-limiting emotions dominate our state of consciousness. This is the cause of all racial and ethnic hatred, as well as much conflict in families.

This kind of a permanent ego-centered reaction can also be related to a specific cause. It is quite possible for us to take a stand for a true cause, but to take this stand based on an ego-centered state of mind and to fight for this cause with impure motives. Once we have decided what we believe to be true, we completely refuse to reconsider the issue and we do not seek to expand our understanding of it—we refuse to grow. The most obvious example is any kind of religious conflict, from outright religious wars to even the most subtle form of judgment or condemnation of another's religion. The belief that "my" religion is the only true one and that all others are wrong is an ego-centered reaction. Only a completely ego-centered person could kill or condemn others in the name of God.

It is extremely important to realize that ego-centered reactions can be very subtle and they will often be disguised as being good. It takes a lot of courage to take an honest look at oneself to evaluate if one's current beliefs are based on a principle- or ego-centered state of consciousness. It also takes a very keen ability to discriminate between the two, and such an ability cannot be developed without work.

CHAPTER 8

The Perspective of Adoption

If we accept the idea that life is a continuum, and that at least some of the things that happen to us in this life could be the effects of causes we set in motion in previous lives, we realize there is a viable alternative to abortion.

When the soul is seen as a continuum, then a child is no longer simply a physical body. The body is a vehicle through which the soul is expressing itself here and now. The soul, the identity of the child, is more than the outer appearance. With this in mind we must rethink our attitude about the relationship between parents and children.

Traditionally, we tend to believe that because the parents give life to their children and give them certain of their attributes, the parents have a certain claim on their children. We all talk about "my" children and we all feel entitled to some kind of return from our children.

As a consequence, we also believe that the child has a certain claim on the parents and the parents have certain obligations to fulfill towards the child. We all say "my" parents and we all feel entitled to something from our parents.

In most Western nations, there has always been a sense of ownership associated with the parent /child relationship. Traditionally, parents could do almost whatever they wanted to their children as long as the children were dependent on them for their sustenance. In Rome, the father had the right to sell the children as slaves. Only a little over a hundred years ago it was common that parents hired their children out for work from a very early age. Child abuse and child molestation were, if not accepted, at least ignored by society.

This attitude is changing. We obviously cannot sell children as slaves nor sell them as workers. Child abuse or molestation has been recognized as a problem society must deal with. Our society is clearly refining its moral and ethical understanding on the subject of how parents and children should relate. This has not, however, been transferred to the unborn child—the parents can still do whatever they want.

We could take this understanding one step further. If the true identity of a child is a soul that is only wearing a particular physical body for this lifetime, then it does not make sense to say that the parents own or have any claim to the child. You cannot own a soul just as you cannot own the former inhabitants of a house when you buy it. Thus, children are not our property; they don't belong to anyone. If we cannot completely disregard the idea that they must belong to someone, then it might be constructive to say they are God's children. Maybe God wants these children to be in embodiment so they can fulfill their mission, do the work He wants them to do for Him and balance their debts to life.

Let us look at another perspective, that of our true identity as a soul that abides in a particular physical body for one single lifetime. How can we claim ownership of this body? If we no longer see the physical body as the totality of our identity, then maybe we should reconsider our claim on it. What if the body is only a loan to us, a gift that we may use for a time to fulfill a certain purpose? Who owns our body, who loaned it to us? Perhaps our body belongs to "Life," to the creative mind or to God. We can name it anything we want. It is obvious that due to the mechanics of the world we live in, bodies do not grow on trees. They come from other bodies as life begets life. Perhaps one of the prices we have to pay to life for the loan of our physical body is that we use it to produce more physical bodies, making it possible for other souls to be part of life on this planet? Possibly we, by denying other souls a body through abortion, will find it difficult to get a body for ourselves after the death of the body we are wearing right now? Is the claim of ownership of "our" body a dangerous illusion that can limit the future freedom of our soul?

By applying the perspective that we do not own children, we begin to question one of the social doctrines of our time, which says you have to take care of your children.

We know that there is a great deal of social pressure put upon new parents. You have to do everything according to an accepted standard put upon you by society and by your own parents. For many young people, especially an unmarried young woman, this can be quite a heavy burden, and there is no question that it weighs heavily in any decision to have an abortion. It seems such an easy way out to have an abortion and get it over with. Having a child binds you for life to a seemingly endless series of restrictions and obligations—or does it? If you do not own the child, then why should you necessarily have to raise it? Could it not be that you could fulfill all obligations to a child by giving it life?

We live in a time in which the knowledge of contraceptive measures, and the contraceptives themselves, are available to all. Could we not consider that by using contraceptive measures a woman is exercising her freedom of choice? If she still becomes pregnant, it could then be seen as an act of fate, of destiny, or as the effect of causes she herself set in motion through exercising her freedom of choice in a past life. In other words, her past choices have now come full circle and have, in a sense, neutralized her present freedom to choose. To fulfill her mission in this life or to pay back a debt to life, she must give birth to the child that is now in her womb. If she does not, she will only further limit her future freedom; whereas by going to term, she can expand her future freedom. Since the pregnancy was unplanned, she has already exercised her freedom of choice about becoming pregnant. That does not mean she has exhausted her freedom of choice. She has a "second line of defense after failed contraception" and her choice is now: Should I choose to raise this child or should I give it up for adoption?

This decision should be very easy, but for many women it is not, and the main reason is social pressure. She doesn't feel she can let go of "her" child, or maybe what she really feels is that society or her parents won't allow her to let go of her child. If she does anyway, she will reap the consequences and maybe become an outcast. It is a peculiar fact, that, for many women in the world today, having an abortion seems more socially acceptable than giving up a child for adoption. Seen from the perspective of the soul, we can see that this attitude is not very loving.

Let us look at the idea that there are a number of souls

waiting to come into embodiment. The causes they set in motion in past lives outline some limitations for when and how they can come into this world. They require a certain set of circumstances to have the best possible opportunity to fulfill their mission and pay back their debt to life. So, when one of these circumstances occurs, the soul is ready and waiting for it. For every woman who ever gets pregnant, there may be a specific soul for whom this pregnancy represents the best possible opportunity for coming into the world.

An abortion terminates this opportunity permanently; it is a definitive measure. The soul may come into embodiment at another time and be born to other parents, but it will never again get the exact same set of circumstances. It may never again be possible for the soul to be born to the same parent. A woman simply cannot have that soul as a child "a couple or years from now when I have finished school."

Adoption is a different story. Now the soul is born in the best possible set of circumstances. It will not be raised by its biological parents, but maybe that is not necessary. The effects from past lives may dictate that the child should be raised by someone else in a different outer framework than it was born in. Sounds complicated? We all know people who are making choices that make their present lives complicated, even chaotic. If they are to reap the consequences of such choices in a future life, that life could also be complicated. If they have used their free will the same way for many past lifetimes, then maybe it is a small wonder their present life is complicated.

We may consider that some people could be infertile as an effect of actions in a past life. At the same time, they could have a debt to pay back to certain other people and this debt could best be paid by acting as the parent for these souls. How could this be accomplished? Adoption could be a key. In other words, seen from a higher perspective of what is best for all parts of life, adoption could be a fully acceptable way for the drama of life to outplay itself. It might allow everyone, the child, the mother and the adoptive parents to win their true soul freedom! It provides a way out for all involved and it is a life-giving solution.

CHAPTER 9

Practical   Solutions

The following suggestions are not chosen because they represent the ultimate solution, but because they are practical. Both
measures are such that hardly anyone can disagree with them
and thus they should be easy to implement.

The Real Freedom of a Real Choice

One of the central themes in the debate has been the pregnant
woman and her freedom of choice. This theme has been the
cause of much conflict, but let us look at some aspects on
which everyone (or almost everyone) can agree. We can all
agree that a democracy should give maximum freedom to the
people. The core of this is that the individual has freedom to
pursue happiness as he or she sees fit. Therefore, when we are
dealing with a pregnant woman, we must consider her as a real
person with real feelings. Our main concern should be her personal happiness, not only right now, but for the rest of her
life. We must, consequently, agree that society should do
everything possible to give the pregnant woman the best possible conditions for making the choice that is right for her personally, a choice she will not regret later. In other words, if
we are truly concerned about a woman's freedom of choice,
let us go all the way to secure that freedom. Anyone with due

respect for other people and their free will must agree to this because anything else would be manipulative.

The fact is—and no one can dispute it—that a number of women have regretted having an abortion. Why would anyone regret having an abortion when they could easily have another child? The explanation is that according to science every human being is a unique individual. There never has been, nor can there ever be, another child with the same individuality, the same combination of genes. Respect for the individual is the basis for our democratic way of life and for all the religions of this world. Only a person with no sensitivity whatsoever towards life could disagree. So, we can conclude that an abortion has certain definitive aspects that cannot be undone or completely compensated for. In other words, if a woman makes the wrong choice and regrets it later, it could be very difficult for her to overcome her grief and sense of loss. The reality of this has been demonstrated in the lives of a number of women. Only a person with no sensitivity for the woman as a real person could ignore this problem. Therefore, we could agree that our society must make sure that when a woman faces the choice to have or not to have an abortion, she will be given the best possible circumstances for making the right choice.

An Informed Choice

Everyone knows that a person can only make a free choice when he or she has as much information as possible about the situation in which the choice has to be made. Therefore, society should make sure that before a woman makes the decision to have or not have an abortion she has been reasonably well informed. Only persons who are seeking to manipulate the woman might disagree.

It is obvious that there is a potential for conflict. We could easily spend another 20 years debating what kind of information a woman should be required to have and how society should make sure she gets it. But actually we don't have to, it really can be very simple. To insure the woman's freedom of choice, the government cannot take a stand on abortion, nor can it define what kind of information would enable her to make the best choice. So, the government cannot give the woman any information because it would be virtually impossible to prevent a subtle manipulation. However, we already have two factions with completely opposite positions on the issue. The truly democratic solution is to require the woman to hear both sides and then allow her to make her own choice. In other words, require the woman to spend one hour with a pro-life center and one hour with a pro-choice center. In that hour, they can tell her whatever they want within the law and the government does not have to censor it or even be concerned about it. We can be sure that the pro-life faction will give her all the reasons why she should not choose an abortion and we can be equally sure that the pro-choice faction will give her all the reasons why she should. In this way she will have heard all the most basic argumentation involved in the debate and thus we must say that she is reasonably well informed.

Is it possible that one or both of the two factions will try to manipulate her? Yes, but since she will hear both sides, it is likely that she will be able to see through it. Furthermore, she will know where each of them is coming from, which is better for her than if she received the information from a seemingly "objective" source such as the government. Is it likely that they will deliberately seek to misinform or scare her? No, because the only way they can hope to influence her decision is to win her trust. If she feels they are trying to scare her, or if she catches them in lying, they will have lost any chance of influencing her decision.

To protect her even more, we could require that she would not be allowed to spend more than one hour on the first visit. If she wanted further counseling, she would not be allowed to come back until the following day. In this way the center would know that she would have time to sleep on the information they give her and that she would only come back if they win her trust. It would therefore be in their own best interest to be truthful and honest with her.

This solution is as close to ideal as it is possible because it should satisfy all the players. The government can feel it has fulfilled its responsibility to protect its citizens, and at the same time, it has allowed both of the warring factions to have their say. Both the pro-life and pro-choice movements will get a chance to influence the woman as they see fit. It cannot be said to be a major inconvenience for a woman to spend two hours obtaining information before making a major decision. So, this solution should satisfy virtually everyone, except the people who do not want the woman to hear the opponent's point of view because they do not want her to make an informed choice.

Protection From Psychological Pressure

When we are under pressure to act within a very short time frame, it becomes more difficult for us to consider our own long-term interests. Almost all of us have made impulsive decisions that we have regretted later. In many forms of sales work, it is common to create a situation in which the customer feels he or she has to act right now or lose an opportunity. The sales person is playing on our fear of loss by making us feel that if we do not buy right now, it will be too late. This is done for the simple reason that it works and gives more sales. Although this is a perfectly legal technique, virtually every state has enacted laws to protect the consumers and give them a way out if they regret the decision. In most states the law says that even if you have signed a legally binding contract, you still have a grace period in which you can cancel the transaction with no penalty whatsoever. Virtually everyone agrees that it is perfectly in order that society seeks to protect us when we are consumers in a sales situation. Thus, everyone can see that this protection should apply to all situations in which people are buying merchandise or a service.

What has this got to do with abortion? When a pregnant woman walks into an abortion clinic, she is a potential buyer of the service the clinic offers. She is, at least in some clinics, confronted with people who are working on a commission basis. The more abortions they sell, the more money they make. One of the basic rules of most types of sales work is to get the customer to make a decision right here and now. Her situation in an abortion clinic is basically the same as when she steps onto a used car lot. The people she meets will see her as a potential customer and they know that no sale means no money. They also know that the best way to sell her is to create a sense of urgency and make her feel she has to make a decision right now, or it will be too late. Women have reported that they have been told that the doctor would go on vacation in a few days and would not return for three weeks. At that time it would be too late to perform an abortion so they had to make up their mind right now. Was the doctor really going on vacation or was this simply a salesman's trick to create urgency and give more sales? The people in the clinic know they can only hope to influence a woman as long as she is in the situation they have created. Any sales person knows that as soon as the customer steps off the lot, he will start rationalizing himself out of the sale.

Anyone who is truly concerned about a pregnant woman as a person should agree that she must be afforded the same protection regarding an abortion, as in any other situation in which she is a consumer. The problem is that once an abortion has been performed it cannot be undone. The only way to protect a woman is to make sure that she has time to think it over before the abortion takes place. Therefore, we should be able to agree that a woman should be required to wait a certain time from the moment she realizes she is pregnant, until she can have an abortion. How long should it be? Why not leave it to the individual states and let it depend on how long a grace period the state laws call for in other situations? Anything less than 24 hours would not give the woman a proper chance to consider her situation. If state law gives a grace period of three to seven days, why not let that be the time.

Yes, of course, certain people will argue that a waiting period can endanger the woman's life, but this is not a valid reason for leaving out the waiting period. The abortion industry keeps telling us how safe even abortion in midterm is, so in 98% of the cases, one to three days will not make a difference. It should be possible to set up a system that could get doctors involved, so a woman could get an abortion sooner if there were medical reasons for it.

Note that some publicly known people have declared that they see no need for, or are directly opposed to, a waiting period before an abortion, yet the same people favor a week-long waiting period before anyone can buy a handgun.

The Question of Counseling

If we are truly concerned about the woman not regretting her choice, there is one more factor we must consider. It is a natural human tendency, when we are faced with an important choice, to talk it over with somebody else. The core of this desire is an inner knowledge that telling our situation to someone else will give us a clearer perspective on it. Sharing our problems with someone else takes some of the emotional pressure off our shoulders. We also have the chance of getting feedback on the situation, giving us knowledge that we may have overlooked. We know that it is quite often difficult for us to make right choices when under pressure, because being involved in the situation makes it impossible for us to consider it objectively. Therefore, most people have a natural desire to get the outside perspective on their situation, and the normal way to do that is to talk it over with someone.

Since the woman herself may be distressed, and therefore not quite able to consider her own long-term interests, it is not unreasonable for society to require her to seek the advice of someone else before she can have an abortion. This is a measure only people who desire to manipulate the woman might disagree with.

The big question here is who that someone should be? Should family members be involved for minors? Should the child's father be involved? Again, we have the potential for much conflict, but the simple solution is to let the woman make her own choice.

There are many qualified counselors and psychologists, who would, no doubt, add abortion counseling to their repertoire. If the woman cannot afford the fee, some counselors may even be willing to do it for free or perhaps society could pay for it. Otherwise, both the pro-life and pro-choice movements would offer free counseling. Would such counseling be objective? No, probably not, but the woman would be well aware of this. She would have spent one hour with each of the two factions, and if she chose one of them for further counseling, it would be because she felt comfortable with them. It is true that such an arrangement might negate the rights of parents or spouses. But in a counseling situation, the most important consideration is that the woman feels comfortable with the counselor. If she does not feel she can discuss the matter with her parents or spouse, it could be very counterproductive to require this by law. If the counselor is a true professional, he or she will recommend that the woman involve parents and spouse where appropriate. It could also be required that the counseling involved subjects such as the possibility for adoption and support-groups that can help the woman during pregnancy or after an abortion.

We are talking about a three-step program.

1. When a woman finds out she is pregnant, she must wait 24 to 72 hours before an abortion can be performed, unless this would endanger her life.

2. Within this waiting period she is required to attend a one hour—no more, no less—information session with a pro-choice and a pro-life center. They can offer her further counseling, but she is not allowed to accept this offer until the following day.

3. Before the abortion is performed, she must document that she has consulted a counselor, and that the session involved certain subjects relevant to her situation (such as parents or spouse).

It may be necessary to create a government agency to control this process and make sure all steps are performed by walking the woman through them. It may be necessary to prevent both pro-life and pro-choice centers from performing pregnancy tests and let this be done on neutral ground.

Is this an ideal arrangement? No, but it is far, far better than the situation a pregnant woman is facing today. Nobody in the pro-choice movement can object to such a proposal, because it simply goes all the way to secure that the woman is making the right choice. Nobody in the pro-life movement should object either, because if their claims are correct, this measure should reduce the number of abortions. When this reduction happens through the woman's free choice, who could possibly object to it?

Ask the People!

We should all be able to agree that in a democracy, government policy should ideally reflect the will of the majority of the
people. We must always be on a quest to make sure that there
is the smallest possible discrepancy between the will of the
people and the policy of the government. For practical reasons, it is impossible to have the people involved with all
government decisions. Therefore, the people elect representa-
tives who set policies and make daily decisions. This system
is both necessary and practical, but perhaps we could consider
that it might have certain limitations. Maybe there are certain
situations in which it cannot guarantee that the will of the
people is reflected in government policy.

We noted earlier that democracy is a means of resolving
human conflict in a peaceful way. If this is so, then democracy
obviously has not been working in the case of abortion, because we have neither resolution nor peace. One reason for
this could be that, so far, the main decision in the abortion
issue has been made by a handful of Supreme Court judges.
These judges are not elected directly by the people, and even if
they were, how could the decision of a handful of people be
representative of 250 million Americans?

It is necessary to have a narrow body that can make decisions regarding the many questions that come up in a large
nation, but maybe this system does not work in all cases.
Abortion is obviously not an ordinary case for the Supreme
Court or for the President or Congress. It is an issue that
involves fundamental moral and ethical questions for which a
clear-cut answer cannot always be given. Maybe such fundamental issues should not be decided by a very narrow body,
but by a far larger group, such as all voters?

America is the world's first democracy, but it is also a very
young nation. It was not a nation before it became a democracy. However, in many other countries the people lived under tyrannical rulers before the advent of democracy. Perhaps
this has given certain experiences that could be helpful when it
comes to an issue like abortion?

In Switzerland, almost all major decisions are made
through a public vote. The Swiss have developed a very
sophisticated system that even allows people to vote by telephone. While such a system may not be practical in a large

nation, we could look for a more moderate version. In Denmark, for example, the constitution opens up the possibility for a public vote in certain cases. The prime minister can call for such a referendum and so can two-thirds of the members of parliament. In the summer of 1992, the Danes voted on the country's participation in the European common market, and much to everyone's surprise, the people voted against government policy. This could provide a solution to the conflict over abortion. Come to think of it, what could be more democratic than letting the people decide on abortion through a direct vote? Who could possibly object to this idea except the kind of people who do not want to follow the will of the people, but want to use the issue to promote a hidden agenda. The question is, will these persons risk exposing themselves by openly opposing a public vote on abortion?

Could such an idea be implemented? No doubt, and if it is preceded by a public debate that seeks to find a new truth based on higher principles, then maybe a real resolution could be achieved. If a large majority of the population voted "yes" or "no" to abortion, the minority should respect this choice as the price we all have to pay to uphold a free democracy.

The only drawback to this idea is that it would no doubt take considerable time to implement it, but on the other hand if we allow the debate to continue on its present track, we may never find a resolution.

The Final Word

Please note that it is not the purpose of this book to say that if we did engage in a search for a spiritual understanding, we would inevitably end up banning abortion. If we did engage in a truly sincere and honest search for a new and higher spiritual understanding, only one thing is certain: We would increase our understanding of life and that would allow us to approach our many problems in a new way. We are likely to find solutions to the many apparently unsolvable problems and these solutions would be based on knowledge rather than guesswork. When it comes to abortion, a higher spiritual understanding could still give us several options.

A lot of Americans might develop the understanding that abortion limits a woman's potential for spiritual development. If so, then laws could be enacted that would require a woman to have a basic knowledge of the spiritual consequences before she could have an abortion. It might even become acceptable for everyone to protect women against the spiritual consequences of abortion, as we protect people today from the consequences of drunk driving.

We may find that abortion has an aftermath, not only for the individual, but perhaps even for a nation as a whole. Could 25 million abortions have created a spiritual debt for the entire nation? If so, we may decide that abortion cannot be left to individual choice because the consequences affect us all.

We may realize that when all is said and done, free will must be treated with ultimate respect in a democratic nation. Perhaps we will gain the knowledge that if a woman is fully aware of all the consequences of an abortion, and is willing to bear the effects, then society should not prevent her from making this choice.

No one can say what we will find on such a spiritual search. But at least we will have done what Columbus did, set out to prove that the earth is round instead of just talking about it. Who knows, we might even rediscover America, the spiritual America, along the way!

PART FOUR

Miscellaneous Forbidden Questions

About Part Four

What you have read up to this point is the main thesis of the book. While I was researching for the book, I came across a lot of material that is not directly related to parts one through three. Since one of my goals is to question a number of our paradigms, I found it natural to include this material. Part Four is therefore a catalogue of different ideas that are not necessarily related to each other or to the first three parts of the book.

CHAPTER 10

A Historical Parallel to The Abortion Debate

The philosopher George Santayana said that if we refuse to learn from the mistakes of the past, we are condemned to repeat those mistakes. So it is logical to ask if there is anything in history that resembles the situation we are facing in the abortion issue? The abortion debate has been called the "clash of absolutes" because it sets two fundamental rights up against each other: the right of the unborn child to live and the right of the woman to make choices about her own body.

In our society we have not found a common ground to resolve this conflict and bridge the gap. We might ask ourselves if the conflict over abortion really is a clash of absolutes or if it only seems like it because we are viewing it from a given perspective? In other words, would the conflict be looked at the same way in any other society or at any other time? Or, is it a set of conditions in our particular society and time that makes it seem as if there is no resolution? We could start by asking how the American society of a century ago would have looked at such a conflict.

A little over a hundred years ago the United States was facing the worst conflict in its short history: the Civil War. The issue of slavery divided our nation in what, at the time, seemed like a clash of absolutes. Because slavery has been abolished in our part of the world for several generations, we tend to view it as the result of a more primitive culture and time. We tend to believe that slavery is a thing of the past.

Could this be the explanation why no one, after 20 years, has pointed out the obvious parallel between the Civil War and the present abortion debate?

What Is Slavery?

Slavery is not a new phenomenon on this planet, it has been around as long as recorded history. The ancient Egyptians and Chinese had slaves. The Babylonians and Romans had slaves and so did the Stone Age cultures of northern Europe. Throughout the Middle Ages, slavery was the order of the day. In fact, during most of what we call the Dark Ages, the majority of the population were the slaves of the king and noble class, the power elite. Any common man or woman was, from his or her birth, the actual property of the nobleman on whose land the parents lived. The common people had to live where their master decided, and they had to work his farmland for as long as he wanted and for a pay that he alone determined.

There has always been a drive, a force, to turn the majority of the human population into slaves of a small group or power elite. There is nothing sophisticated or political about this observation, it is a simple matter of applying common sense to what we all know about history.

Now, just as there is a drive to enslave other people, there is also a drive to free them. Again, we can easily observe from history that there has always been a force seeking to give freedom to every human being. This force has been working to bring forth the ideas that would create a society to guarantee "life, liberty and the pursuit of happiness" for all. Such a society did not become a reality until the modern democracies were established some 200 years ago, though we can trace the efforts to establish greater freedom back throughout recorded history. The philosophical basis for ending slavery had evolved gradually over thousands of years. Bringing forth a society with greater freedom is an ongoing, but slow process. As a result of this drive for improvement, most people will probably agree that mankind is engaged in a constant movement toward greater and greater freedom.

One result of this progression toward freedom is that we are constantly refining our moral and ethical understanding. What was considered normal and acceptable in the past may be considered crude and primitive today. In our present society, it is self-evident to almost everyone that slavery is not acceptable. This is something we don't even think about and we could never have a public debate about whether one person can own another person. Yet only a little over a hundred years ago, such a debate deeply divided the United States and the division was great enough to make the two opposing sides resort to violence.

Because the two opposing sides were ready to go to war over this issue, it shows clearly that those who were for slavery had a very strong belief in their right to hold slaves. They were ready to go to the ultimate extreme to maintain that right. The feelings for maintaining slavery were at least as strong as the feelings involved in today's abortion debate. From our viewpoint today, it seems unimaginable that anyone could ever have had such feelings. We cannot understand how the issue of slavery could lead to a civil war. We certainly wouldn't have had to go to such an extreme to end slavery, but we are already sliding into a similar conflict over the issue of abortion. It may not escalate into a full-scale civil war, but once you open the Pandora's box of violence, no one can tell just how far it will go.

We should consider that before the Civil War the debate about slavery seemed to the early Americans to be as much a clash of absolutes as the debate on abortion seems to us today. As a result of the moral and ethical understanding of that time, our forefathers were unable to resolve the issue of slavery peacefully. Is it because of limitations in our moral and ethical understanding that we apparently cannot come to a peaceful resolution of the abortion issue today? How will society look upon the abortion debate a century from now? Will society have developed a moral and ethical understanding that makes the resolution to the abortion issue as self-evident to them as the slavery issue now seems to us? If so, could we not today try to get a glimpse of what this expanded understanding might be like? To do so would most certainly help us develop a new approach to the issue.

Let's continue with the issue of slavery for a bit because there is more we can learn from it. What we sometimes tend to forget is that the conflict over slavery took place in a democratic nation. The United States is the prime example of a democracy. The U. S. Constitution is looked upon as a prototype for all democratic constitutions. It is a groundbreaking document based on deep spiritual insights and a far-reaching knowledge of what is the reality of human existence. When one reads the Constitution, it seems unbelievable that a conflict over an issue like slavery could escalate into a civil war in a country with such a foundation. How can there be a conflict over slavery when the very basis of the nation is that all men are created equal and endowed by their creator with inalienable rights?

Well, there are two factors to consider in answering this question and they both tie directly into the core of the abortion debate.

Is a "Black" a Person?

The Declaration of Independence and the Constitution guarantee equal rights to all. The Declaration uses the term men and the Constitution uses the term persons. What is a person? Would the plantation owners of the South have held white people as slaves? Probably not. Slavery was never generally accepted as a principle in the United States, neither in the North nor in the South. Slavery was, even then, looked upon as a thing of the past, the result of a non-democratic society with a more primitive moral standard. Most of the people who bought black Africans to work on their farms did not believe they had bought slaves. Why not? Because they did not believe that a black African was a person! This may seem shocking today, but it was true for a majority of slaveholders. There were people in those days who did not consider blacks as persons protected by the Constitution.

Today, one of the fundamental questions in the abortion debate is whether a fetus is a person. Many people who in our society are considered to be the intellectual elite—scholars, lawmakers and other experts—are seriously debating whether an unborn can be considered a person. As was said earlier, the human intellect can turn anything into a relative issue with pros and cons. In the past, the same kind of people were debating whether a black African was a person.

If a fetus is considered to be a person, it is automatically protected by the Constitution and will have the rights defined in that document. The same is true of blacks. If they had been accepted as persons and been protected by the Constitution, that would have ended slavery. Is that why some people held on to the idea that blacks were not people? Could that be why they did not really want to find an answer to the question and why they held on to this belief even long after the Civil War was over? Could this be the reason we still have racial conflicts today?

Why have we been unable to resolve the question of whether a fetus is a person? Is it because we also have a reluctance toward finding the answer? If the established positions cannot give us a deeper understanding of just when a fetus becomes a person, should we not look beyond those positions?

Can People Be Owned as Property?

The second element we have to consider as being at the core of both the slavery and abortion issues is property rights. Let us first consider why there are property rights. In feudal Europe there were property rights, but they were not equal rights. The king and the noble class could take whatever property they wanted and get away with it. The way to resolve a dispute over property was often an armed conflict, with the stronger side ending up with the goods. This is "the law of the jungle" or the "might is right" principle. Democracy replaces this by defining the means for how one can acquire property and by upholding the right to keep that which you own legally. Democracy also guarantees that no one can interfere with what you do with your property as long as you follow the law. Men with more money or more muscle cannot take your holdings away from you. The right to private property is one of the cornerstones of democracy. Without property rights, there would be no democracy. Our society would inevitably slide into either total anarchy (which is simply another word for "might is right") or totalitarianism (meaning that a central power, the state, owns all property).

With this in mind, we can clearly see why the conflict over slavery escalated into a civil war. The plantation owners of the South had a constitutional right to their private property and to do with it as they saw fit. Slaves were part of their property because, at the time, there was simply no way to run the plantations without them. The slaves were bought through a perfectly legal process, and then suddenly somebody up north claimed to have the higher moral ground. The existence of the Northerners would not have been threatened by the abolishment of slavery, but the private property rights of the Southerners would. When viewed from this perspective, it is no wonder that the conflict over slavery seemed insoluble at the time.

Today, of course, we have a deeper moral understanding. We clearly recognize that a living person cannot be considered property, and therefore the idea of property rights does not apply to people. We could never have a debate over such an issue—or could we?

If an unborn fetus is not a person, then what is it? If not a person, it must be a thing and thus subject to the private property rights guaranteed by the Constitution. Most people will agree that according to the Constitution, persons are the only "objects" that are not subject to private property rights. Is that why some pro-choice proponents claim abortion should be respected as part of our right to privacy? Isn't the core of the right to privacy that people have private property and can do with it what they want without interference from anyone?

Almost everyone will agree that our society cannot uphold the right to privacy if it violates or destroys another person's right to life. You cannot own other people and you cannot do whatever you want to them and then claim it is part of your right to privacy. There is a growing awareness in our society that parents cannot do what they want to their children, not even in the privacy of their own home.

The only way abortion can be considered as part of a woman's right to privacy is if the fetus is not a person. In other words, if a woman owns an unborn child, she can do whatever she wants with it. Or we could say that because the fetus is considered to be a part of the woman's body and because she owns her body, the fetus comes under her right to privacy. This leaves us with the following two options.

If our society, sometime in the future, evolves to a moral understanding that a fetus is not a person, then this position will have stood the test of time. But if society has developed an understanding that a fetus is a person, then some pro-choice people are taking the same position today as the slaveholders did in the Civil War. If a black is not a person, he or she can be owned; and if a fetus is not a person, he or she can be owned as well.

CHAPTER 11

How Ideas Grow

The British historian Arnold Toynbee spent a lifetime studying what causes the rise and fall of civilizations. He said that all societies will be influenced by an elite and he discriminated between two forms of elites, a creative minority and a dominant minority. If the creative minority is allowed to lead, then a civilization will flourish and grow to great heights. If the dominant minority takes over, and they are always trying which is why he called them dominant, then society will begin to disintegrate and will often self-destruct.

The idea of the two opposing elites has a number of parallels and I believe we could benefit from taking a brief look at them. Toynbee's creative minority seems to correspond to what Stephen Covey calls principle-centered leaders and I call them people driven by enlightened self-interest. The dominant minority are the ego-centered leaders or what I call the power elite. I believe Scott Peck is calling this type of persons "the people of the lie." Another parallel is Erich Fromm's concepts of the biophiliac and the necrophiliac, developed from his study of nazism. According to Fromm, we all have two opposing tendencies in our psychology; the biophilic tendency is a love for life and the necrophilic is an attraction to death, which I see as a refusal to grow. A necrophiliac is a person who looks upon other people as things or objects that can be used or destroyed in the fulfillment of a personal desire. According to Fromm, necrophiliacs can only relate to other people if they themselves are in complete control; they literally want to own others. You can only control others if you can predict their reactions and since people are unpredictable, the necrophiliac seeks to reduce them to mechanical entities, a kind of robot, that can be managed as things. Necrophiliacs have an insatiable need for power and they will do almost anything to get it. The trademark of a necrophiliac is that the ends can justify the means. To me this sounds like a person who has become extremely ego-centered.

When I was younger, one of my most basic paradigms stated that power-hungry people simply could not operate in a democracy. I knew that in any other type of society, including many of the totalitarian nations in today's world, this type of people have the upper hand, but in a democracy they didn't have a chance. I apparently must have believed that these people evaporated into thin air when the Declaration of Independence was signed. It was rather painful for me to give up this paradigm and the feeling of security that went with it.

What finally caused me to let go was the following realizations: it dawned on me that a democracy really did not make it impossible for power-hungry people to operate; it only changed the rules of the game. In a totalitarian society the power elite seeks to gain control through physical force and fear. This is actually a very crude way of seeking to dominate others, because the victims will always feel they are being suppressed. As a result they have a longing for freedom and sooner or later they will revolt against their oppressors. The really smart way to dominate others is to make them believe in a set of ideas that are distorted by ego-centered motives. In this way it is possible to make people believe that it is in their own best interest, or at least the lesser evil, for them to be ruled by a small elite. In that situation people may not even realize they are oppressed and they will probably never try to escape the bonds. An iron chain is a primitive way to bind someone, it is much more efficient to use a false idea.

I then realized that a democracy is more vulnerable to the deceptive use of false ideas than any other type of society. Why? Let us consider how we can prevent false ideas from being used to enslave our minds. We must do three things:

    1. We must create a standard for evaluating which ideas are deceptive and which are not.

2. In order to be effective, such an evaluation would have to be done by a centralized authority.

3. We would have to set up a police force that could enforce the judgments made by the central authority.

These three measures are not difficult to implement; there is just one little problem. Each one of them goes against the fundamental principles that a democracy is founded upon. In a democracy all persons have complete freedom to believe in anything they want and they also have the right to express their ideas in public. So, any attempt to evaluate ideas would lead to state control of every aspect of our lives and then we no longer have a democracy, but a society that resembles George Orwell's vision from his book *1984*. The most powerful institution in Orwell's society is a Thought Police seeking to control the innermost thoughts of the people. The conclusion I make is that it is fundamentally impossible to protect a democratic society against subversion by false ideas. Ego-centered people can freely promote any false idea they want since their right to do so is guaranteed by the Constitution.

A New Look at History

To me these realizations represented a major paradigm-shift that virtually revolutionized my way of thinking. I began to see that the concept of certain people using false ideas to attain power could give me a new and deeper understanding of history. It allowed me to understand why so many originally constructive efforts ended up in disaster and I began to see a pattern. In most cases a new endeavor, be it an entire civilization or an organization, will start out with a very constructive foundation of principles. In the beginning most of the leaders belong to the creative minority and are principle-centered people. As soon as the organization has grown to such a size that it begins to have considerable influence upon society, a new type of people will become attracted to it. These are the ego-centered people and they do not join the organization because they believe in its original purpose, they simply want to use the organization as a vehicle for attaining personal power. These necrophiliacs will use all means available to them to get that power and they will often challenge the original leaders. It is very important to understand that whenever there is a power-struggle between an ego-centered and a principle-centered person, the necrophiliac automatically has the upper hand. An ego-centered person will lie and compromise principles to get his way, whereas a principle-centered person never compromises principles to get or maintain personal power. History is littered with examples of how necrophiliacs have dethroned more principle-centered leaders. As soon as these people begin to gain influence in an organization, they will gradually create a situation in which it becomes necessary to compromise principles in order to gain influence. The author Antony C. Sutton states that the result is "you gotta go along to get along," meaning that if you are not willing to compromise principles, you will find it very difficult to stay in the organization. Through this process all the principle-centered leaders will gradually be filtered out and the organization is now entirely in the hands of the necrophiliacs. From then on a phase-transition occurs and the organization will be transformed into a machine with the sole purpose of maintaining and expanding the personal power of the leaders.

It should be obvious that I believe this mechanism has influenced the evolution of the Christian churches, but I think it also accounts for some of the problems we see in modern democracies. I have met many people who believe politics have gotten so dirty that they don't want to have anything to do with it. Well, if a lot of principle-centered people withdraw from politics, what kind of people will be left to run society?

The only way to prevent the subversion of a democracy is that a vast majority of the people develop their inherent ability to discriminate between ideas that are influenced by the human ego and ideas based on timeless principles. In a democracy it is a basic necessity that we the people, consciously and actively seek to establish a clear telephone line to our discriminating self. I believe this is why one of the early presidents said that our constitution will only work for moral and religious people. If we do not fulfill that responsibility, then the democratic process will inevitably begin to break down and our society will become influenced by a dominant minority. It only takes good men doing nothing for evil to triumph.

I think a lot of Americans are beginning to realize that something has gone wrong in our nation. Unfortunately, most people have not yet understood that the real problem is that all of us, that means you, I and all the rest, have let go of our responsibility to discriminate. Until we make a conscious decision to pick up that responsibility and look beyond our existing paradigms for a new and higher understanding, all talk about change will make little difference.

I would like to make it very clear that my purpose for bringing up the subject of a power elite is not to give us an easy way out. I am not trying to find a scapegoat that we can blame for all our problems. Nor am I trying to say that the abortion debate is controlled by an elite. The subject of a power elite is very delicate and it is extremely important that we do not start a witch-hunt. Once again, we must never turn other people into enemies. It is my opinion that the vast majority of the people who are acting as, or supporting a power elite, are not evil at all. So, why are they seeking to dominate society? Because they have come to believe in a set of false ideas and, as before, we see that the real enemy of freedom and democracy is the false idea.

This brings us back to the human ego and its need for self-justification, which explains why so many ego-centered people feel a strong need to convert others. The result is that throughout history a number of ego-centered people have written down their ideas and launched them as a new religious, political or scientific theory. I believe a few of these people have deliberately formulated false ideas, but the majority of them were simply trapped by the workings of their own egos. They really believed their theories would be for the benefit of humankind. Most of the people who picked up the new theory likewise lacked the discrimination to see the ego-centered influence, but there was always a minority who only accepted the theory because is suited their own purposes. In a centralized society, a very small group of people can elevate a false idea to government policy, but this can also happen in a democracy. It is also possible that our democratic societies could have inherited a set of false ideas from the past. These ideas could have been around for so long that we never get around to questioning them. As an example of how ego-centered ideas can survive for a very long time, I would like to use the thoughts expressed in this chapter as the basis for examining one of the major forces in the abortion debate.

Before I leave the subject of elites, let me mention that I have met many people who are very open to the thought that a democratic nation can be influenced by an elite. Others completely refuse to consider it even as a theoretical possibility. For anyone interested in the subject, there are a number of books that give a much more detailed description of elite influences than I have given here. Some of the more general books are, *The Irony of Democracy* by Thomas R. Dye and Harmon Zeigler and, *Who Rules America Now?* by G. William Domhoff. There are also books dealing with a more organized elite effort. One is, *The Naked Capitalist* by Skousen. Also the British author Antony C. Sutton has written almost twenty books on the subject. Some of his titles are: *An introduction to the Order* and *How the Order Creates War and Revolution*. If you are wondering why you never heard about the subjects of a power elite and false ideas in school, you might want to read Sutton's book, *How the Order Controls Education.*

The History of Overpopulation

When I was a teenager, I was extremely concerned about environmental problems. I was convinced that pollution was the most severe threat humankind was facing and that it would no doubt kill us all sooner rather than later. I was equally convinced that the cause of pollution was very easy to define; there were simply too many people on this planet. Overpopulation was the cause of not only environmental problems, but a host of other problems as well.

At the time, I was not concerned about the abortion issue, but if I had been, I am sure I would have looked at abortion as a reasonable way to combat the overpopulation problem. I think this is a very important point to bring up because the idea of overpopulation is a hidden, but very powerful factor in the abortion debate. Over the past three decades all Western democracies have been exposed to a very intense media-campaign focusing on environmental problems. As a result, a great number of people have, as did I, come to believe that overpopulation is one of the major problems facing mankind. This has caused some people, who would otherwise be against abortion for moral reasons, to accept it as a lesser of two evils. If the choice is between large numbers of abortions or mass-starvation, then abortion seems like a more humane alternative. However, is that really the only choice we have and is the earth really overpopulated?

Let me explain what caused me to begin to question my paradigm of overpopulation. First of all I realized that what some people in the environmental movement have been doing since the early '60s bears a striking resemblance to what the Catholic church did in Medieval Europe. Some environmentalists have repeated the church's attempts to rule through guilt and fear, and as a result we have all been exposed to a modern version of the concept of original sin.

Many animal species can greatly transform their environment. For example African elephants knock down young trees to eat their leaves and thereby serve to prevent the savannas from growing into forest. Many native peoples do the same thing. In his book *Playing God in Yellowstone*, Alston Chase argues that the prairies of North America were most likely created by native Americans who deliberately burned down the forests. The reason being that open grassland can sustain larger populations of game animals than old-growth forest. To some environmentalists the changes created by animals and natives are quite natural, but any change created by industrialized man is immediately a threat to the ecosystem. This will inevitably destroy the so-called balance of nature and threaten our survival as a race.

According to the church we are all descendants of Adam and Eve and since they were cast out of Paradise, we are born as sinners. The only way to escape this original sin is to follow the rules defined by the church. According to some environmentalists, modern industrialized man is a sinner by his very existence and the only way out is to follow the recommendations of the environmental movement.

I want to make it clear that I am not trying to say that we do not have environmental problems, we most certainly do. Nor am I trying to knock the entire environmental movement. I am simply pointing out that guilt and fear have been a part of the environmental debate from day one and that it has caused a great number of people to see themselves as sinners against nature. I don't think this attitude will help solve the environmental problems because it is an open invitation to political manipulation.

The second factor that caused me to question the overpopulation paradigm was the realization that overpopulation is not a new idea. I thought it was a concept that had arisen in this century, but certain people have been talking overpopulation for 400 years. This shows how an idea that was created by a power elite in Medieval Europe can survive to the present day and have a major impact on our democratic debate.

The Preformation Theory

The idea that the world could be overpopulated really began in the 1600s as the so-called preformation theory. The concept was that human beings (and animals, for that matter) were preformed in microscopic size even before conception. After conception, they grew and grew until they reached adult size. This theory influenced the philosophical beliefs of the noble class and the budding scientific establishment—which we could call the power elite of the time. Why was this theory so appealing to this class of people? Because it stated that even before conception it was determined by nature what a person's physical and psychological characteristics would be. Thus, it was predetermined who were to become rich and powerful and who were to become poor. The division of society into a rich and powerful minority and a poor, subdued majority was seen as an act of nature herself.

It should be no surprise that such a theory had wide appeal to elitists, simply looking to nature for a justification of their wealth and power, as well as the poverty of those below them. Their reasoning was that since some people were obviously more powerful than others, nature must have ordained it, and it was fully justified that the elite took privileges from the people. The elite had a right to subdue the masses and the masses had no right to resist.

The theory of preformation would probably have been short-lived if it had not been for a professor in anatomy from Bologna named Marcello Malpighi. He was a respected scientist who had made several important discoveries with his microscope. One fine day in 1672, he examined an egg that he believed to be neither fertile nor incubated, but unknown to him, it had been left out in the sun.

Inside, he discovered a well-developed chick embryo. To him, this was proof that a preformed embryo was present from the moment the egg was formed. Because of this and other similar "discoveries" by other scientists who claimed to have seen complete preformed humans inside spermatozoan, the preformation theory survived. In the early 1700s, it was a well-established "scientific fact."

At the time, there was no knowledge of cells and it took almost another century before the idea was developed that every cell comes from a parent cell. It was not until the middle of the 19th century that scientists finally disproved the preformation theory.

The reason we need to consider the preformation theory is that it demonstrates that there was a very strong belief in an "inevitable" division of society into two classes. The elite had a strong belief that the quality of the race as a whole could be maintained by controlling which segments of the population were allowed to propagate. There was also a widely held belief that only people with "desirable" qualities should be allowed to reproduce. In other words, throughout the Middle Ages, it was seen by the ruling elite as a necessity for the preservation of society to prevent or at least restrict the growth of the lower classes. This can be traced even further back—for example, Julius and Augustus Caesar both offered increasingly large rewards to upper-class families for having children and penalized lower-class families for bearing children. When we understand this drive, this fear, that the "lower classes" could become too numerous, we can better understand what happened in subsequent centuries.

The Birth of the
Age of Overpopulation

The idea of overpopulation was fathered in 1798 when Thomas Malthus published his *Essay on Principles of Population as It Affects Future Improvement of Society*. His theory was that population, if left unchecked, would increase at a geometrical ratio (2 x 2 = 4; 4 x 4 = 16), but the means for keeping the population alive could only be increased at an arithmetical ratio (2 + 2 = 4; 4 + 4 = 8). According to Malthus, it was obvious to anyone with a basic understanding of mathematics, that the population had a potential for increasing much faster than food production. Because it is a law of nature that people have to eat to survive, the growth in population and food supply have to be kept at an even ratio.

Malthus concluded that the faster growth in population would result in the condition of the poor becoming

increasingly hopeless. Unless famine or war interfered to di-
minish the population, the means of life would eventually
prove inadequate. If this sounds like another justification for a
society with a rich minority and a poor majority, it is probably
no coincidence. According to author Allen Chase, Malthus
used a perversion of scientific and historical facts to create a
myth of two distinct races of mankind: the elite and the
masses.

Malthus combined an economic theory with the idea of a
superior elite, and thus created scientific racism. According to
Chase, there was only one purpose for this theory: to preserve
the feudal society.

Malthus argued that the gap between population and food
supply would have to be closed. He then concluded that the
only way to accomplish this was to limit the growth of the
population, that is, the poor part of the population. Malthus's
theory quickly gained wide acceptance among the elite of his
time, and as we shall see later, it is still believed by a great
number of people today. But before we look at the impact of
the theory, let us examine its soundness.

There are several factors that Malthus did not take into consideration. First, history demonstrates that the human population over time does not grow faster than the food supply.
When all people lived in hunter-gatherer cultures, there were
few people on this planet. As demonstrated by the hunter-
gatherer cultures still found today, such a culture simply cannot overpopulate an area. Neither the aborigines in Australia,
the Pygmies in Africa, nor the Eskimos in the Arctic overpopulated their areas.

The world population did not really start growing until
farming was introduced some 8,000 years ago. In the hunter-
gatherer culture, the average life span was very low, child
mortality was high, and as a result, birth rates were high.
When the primitive cultures started tilling the land, the result
was a sudden improvement in living conditions. People lived
longer and more people survived to adulthood. So the population grew rapidly and it is likely that a "population explosion"
occurred. After an initial spurt, which might have caused a
brief overpopulation, an adjustment occurred and birth rates
fell. From that point on, the population grew very gradually as
farming techniques improved and this continued into the Middle Ages. During the Stone, Bronze and Iron Ages in northern
Europe, where Malthus formulated his theory, the growth in

population was not explosive and did not cause a tremendous poverty problem. These societies had privileged leaders and they had slaves, but the majority of the population were not poor.

The problem of a majority of the population living in poverty really did not occur until the feudal societies were formed! When the feudal societies appeared, the gap between rich and poor grew, and more and more wealth was concentrated in the hands of fewer and fewer people. It was this social change that caused the division of society into a rich minority and a majority living in poverty. We see that poverty is not the inevitable result of population growth. Rather, it is the result of a social change in which a small elite assumes greater and greater power and privilege. A quick glance at history should reveal that the main cause of poverty always has been the monopolization of wealth in the hands of an elite.

In the feudal societies, the situation was somewhat similar to that found in a hunter-gatherer culture. The extreme poverty caused high child mortality and a shortened lifespan. As a result, birth rates were high. Then, around Malthus's time, this situation changed dramatically. Better knowledge of health care and hygiene lowered mortality and increased the lifespan. The budding industrial revolution began to raise the standard of living, even for the poor part of the population. Because birth rates do not respond overnight, the population of Europe "exploded."

These events may seem to justify Malthus's conclusions, but we have to consider one more factor. The industrial revolution was in reality also an agricultural revolution. New crops, better farming techniques, better distribution and increased mechanization of farming caused food production to rise dramatically. Indeed, we must conclude that through knowledge and technology, it is quite possible to increase food production geometrically.

Malthus was well aware of this fact, but he nevertheless kept promoting his theory. Also, the power elite of his time gave him all the help they could because it fit their agenda and justified their privileges! This is what Scott Peck describes as a basic characteristic of people of the lie: They insist on "affirmation against all findings."

History Has Proven Malthus Wrong

We might also add that history has clearly proven Malthus wrong. In all the industrialized nations, we have seen the same pattern: As the standard of living increased, the birth rate declined and the population growth gradually came to a halt. In many of the richest nations of the world, the population would actually be declining if it weren't for immigration. We can conclude that the best way to stop population growth is to enact a social change that raises the standard of living. Of course, this would eliminate the privileged elite. The power elite is not trying to stop population growth so much as trying to prevent social change—and they know very well what produces this change: a growing population!

Malthus developed his theories to say that a child of poor parents should not be supported by the state because such a child was of no value to society. He recommended that the state take active measures to make the poor population decrease. Among the measures he recommended were the abandonment of health care and cleanliness for the poor, even the reintroduction of the plague! He developed a truly cold, cunning theory of life, which seems all the more strange considering that Malthus was a minister. This can teach us some important lessons:

1. The theory of the population explosion was never based on scientific facts or on a sound observation of history.

2. It is not a scientific theory, but a political theory designed to prevent social change, that is, the overturning of the power elite.

3. The theory was promoted as an expression of a desire to help the poor, because a growth in the population could only lead to misery, famine, even war. Hence, it became a justification for population control disguised as an unselfish initiative.

4. The theory was formulated in a way that totally obscured the reality of the situation as well as the actual cause of the problem. It was not a growing population

that was the cause of poverty, but the existence of the power elite and their monopolization of wealth.

This shows a very important principle for understanding how a power elite can influence society: First, a power elite causes a problem. When the problem can no longer be ignored, the elite formulates a solution that portrays themselves as saviors of the people.

Darwin and Survival of the Fittest

Malthus had a tremendous influence upon the scientific community of his time—even beyond his time, including Charles Darwin. Darwin is seen by many today as the savior that freed mankind's mind from the tyranny imposed by organized religion. He did so by providing an alternative to the description of creation set forth in the scriptures. What is not so well known is that his most famous book had the full title of *On the Origin of Species by Means of Natural Selection, Or the Preservation of the Favorite Races in the Struggle for Life.* The main purpose of the book was to prove scientifically that it is necessary to preserve the "favorite races."

The influence of Darwin on the elite of his time was great. He had a tremendous influence on the German philosopher Friedrich Nietzsche, who in turn influenced Adolf Hitler.

What is not so well known is that both Darwin and Malthus were greatly influenced by Erasmus Darwin, Charles's grandfather. Charles merely expanded and clarified his grandfather's theory. Hitler's idea of a superior race goes directly back to Erasmus Darwin who had developed his own theory of evolution.

Sir Francis Galton

Another of Erasmus Darwin's grandsons was Sir Francis Galton, the father of modern eugenics—the idea that selective "breeding" can improve the human race. Eugenics, from the Greek, means well born. In reality, it is the science of the superior race. In 1891, Sir Galton was the first to call for forced sterilization of the poor. This ultimately led to forced sterilization of the Jews in Nazi Germany—in order to purify the race.

Sir Galton's first book, *Hereditary Genius*, was published in 1869. It was a statistical study of prominent men, showing that children of rich men were more likely to reach prominent positions in society. Sir Galton believed the cause was "in the blood," completely ignoring the fact that men already in positions of power had all the means necessary to make sure that their own children were favored over others. He also ignored the fact that only the elite had the means to give their children an education.

The Superior Race

Throughout history, there has always been a drive to find proof that there are two distinct races: a superior race with the right to special privileges and an inferior race (the majority of the world's population) whose only justification for existence is that they are needed to do the hard work. When the lower race grows beyond the number needed to uphold the status quo, the elite begins to talk about overpopulation. Suddenly, poor people are considered enemies of the state, acceptable only if they stop multiplying themselves—either through celibacy, sterilization, contraception, or abortion. If they refuse to stop multiplying, then all help should be withdrawn from them and they should be allowed to die, until their numbers have again reached an acceptable level.

One of the people greatly influenced by this concept was Karl Marx. Although he sought to make use of the masses to create political change, he really hated the masses—a fact he never sought to hide in his writings. Not many people are aware of this, because very few people have read his original writings.

These ideas are obviously in total opposition to the Golden Rule. We might therefore ask, what this shows us about these people and their attitude to life? Can such a philosophy be an expression of brotherly love, as it claims to be, or is it a disguised form of hatred for poor people or what I would call normal, loving people.

Social Darwinism: Herbert Spencer

Herbert Spencer was the first to apply Darwin's theories to society in a practical form. His father, William Spencer, was a nonconformist and for many years was secretary of the Derby Philosophical Association, founded by Erasmus Darwin. In one of Herbert's books, *Progress, its Law and Cause* published in 1857, he coined the term *survival of the fittest*, which is usually attributed to Darwin, though his book was published before Darwin's *On the Origin of the Species*. He postulated that the superior race represented the most fit people and therefore had a right to survive that was built into the laws of nature. Accordingly, it would be wrong to help the poor. He said, "The forces that are bringing forth the great scheme of happiness exterminate sections of mankind that stand in their way with the same sternness they exterminate beasts of prey or useless species." In other words, the elite should simply let this lower class die.

According to Spencer, an unknown force was working on the human population to secure the survival of the most fit, the elite. He believed that the social order evolved like the natural order. Thereby, he applied the principle of biological evolution to the social sphere and created Social Darwinism.

In the late 1800s, his theories were used to justify the position of the elite as an expression of natural law and gained widespread popularity. Progress was defined as a process of purifying society from the unfit, the lower social classes. Spencer's theories became especially popular among the big businessmen of the time, who were feverishly seeking to form trusts to create business monopolies. For John D. Rockefeller, the growth of a large business and the deliberate elimination of other businesses through any available means was simply the process of survival of the fittest. For him it was the working out of the laws of nature, the laws of God or the supreme force.

Scientific Racism

In reality racism may not be a discrimination based on outer, physical characteristics such as skin color. It seems like some people want to create a race within the race, an elite with a right to hold superior privileges. Racism is also the desire of the power elite to justify its position as being the result of a natural process created by God.

We can see that the idea of survival of the fittest in the social sphere is really based on flawed reasoning. The basis for the formulation of the idea is a fear that the lower classes will become so numerous that they will force a change that causes the elite to lose its privileges. If this happened it should, according to the theory, simply be the result of a natural process. If the poor took power from the elite, it would show that they had become more fit than the elite and it would only be natural for them to take over. In the animal kingdom, there is an ongoing process in which new species develop that are more fit than existing species and eventually replace them. Thus, it should only be natural that there was a turnover in the social sphere.

If the power elite really believed in this theory, they should simply let nature run its course. If their ideas were correct, the lower classes should eliminate themselves. Instead, the power elite, to the present day, has sought to justify the idea that the state has to give nature a helping hand in eliminating the lower classes through sterilization, birth control and abortion. This completely illogical reasoning is very typical for "people of the lie," who are always seeking to come up with a logical, factual rationale for justifying what they want to accomplish right now. When their goals change, their rationale will change with them, because all people of the lie are humanists. They believe man has the right to define reality according to his immediate desires.

What we must understand is that a society functioning after this ego-centered rationale simply cannot survive in the long run because it is not "fit" enough. Only a society based on timeless principles can survive.

Scientific Fatalism

Darwin was not the first to come up with the theory of evolution. In the late 1800s, many scientists and philosophers, including Karl Marx, firmly believed that history had already proven that man did not need to be dependent on God, that he could establish his own laws and create a society that would go on without God.

Darwin's theory was based on hindsight and it is not necessarily logical. In our society, we have been programmed to believe that life evolved from fish to reptiles, from reptiles to mammals, and from mammals to man. But observing a fish gives no basis for concluding that evolution "automatically" produced man from it. This is not logic in a higher sense, but merely intellectual reasoning that has to define everything within a relative framework. This is because the intellect cannot fathom the idea that the physical creation could be effects of causes on a higher level of existence. Even if the species are the result of an evolutionary process, how can this disprove the influence of a higher mind, a directing intelligence working from a higher level of existence?

What is even less logical is the idea that social progress in a human society should follow the same pattern as that of so-called biological evolution. Yet this idea is widely accepted today because it fits the cause of the power elite. According to social Darwinism, there are classes in society, just like in the animal kingdom, with the elite as the highest class and the poor majority as the lowest class.

In a sense, this could be called *scientific fatalism*, in which Darwin's terms of heredity and environment are the only determining factors, completely replacing free will as a factor in individual and social life. However, it only replaces the free will of the masses and not of the power elite. The elitists believe they are driven by the highest drive in life, the "will to overpower," which is what causes the more-fit to take dominion. Is this a clever attempt to make the majority of the population abstain from using their free will by turning it over to the power elite? We know that the ideas of heredity and environment have become almost universally accepted in our society. They have been infused into our entire educational establishment and thereby influence the thoughts of nearly everyone in very subtle ways. This tends to limit people by holding back their creativity and will.

This elitist idea completely denies the fact that history has delivered numerous examples of how individuals have used their will to rise over both hereditary and environmental circumstances. It also denies that it is always an individual who provides the impetus for change. Is it an attempt to turn the majority of the population into "social animals," with no individual creativity or will? Such a population would not be able to lead any society, they would have to allow an elite to make all the decisions for them as in *Brave New World* by Aldous Huxley.

The Birth of Birth Control

Next in line to pick up where Darwin and Spencer left off was Margaret Sanger, often seen as the hero of the modern birth control movement. She started her career by advocating abortion, but influential friends soon made her realize that she was too far ahead of her time. Instead, she began to portray herself as the defender of the poor woman, with the goal of setting her free from the drudgery of having so many children. Sanger accomplished this goal through the means of birth control. What did she see as the essence of birth control? In 1919, she wrote that birth control means "more children from the fit and fewer children from the unfit."

This quotation describes what is and always has been the driving force behind birth control, but these eugenicist viewpoints are virtually unknown in the abortion debate of today. The term birth control says it all. Someone is obviously in control, but the question is who—the fit or the unfit, the people or the power elite?

In 1927, Sanger organized the first world population conference, which led directly to forced sterilization of those deemed unfit by the ruling elite. Sanger was tied in with the eugenics movement, which in turn was intertwined with the most wealthy and most powerful people of the time. John D. Rockefeller was one of the most influential people in the population movement. Sanger often turned to him for financing and he was instrumental in the launching of the population control movement.

The means for discriminating between the fit and the unfit is their position on the social ladder, their wealth or lack of it.

The poor are always deemed unfit. But why are they poor? They are poor because of the manipulation of power by a small elite leading to an unjust distribution of wealth and privileges! Again, we see the principle where the power elite, in its desire to gain privileges, creates an imbalance in society. When this imbalance can no longer be ignored, the elitists propose a solution that makes them appear as saviors. They also manage to obscure the real alternative: to educate the poor and bring us back to a free-market economy with equal opportunities for all. We see that the modern abortion movement is building directly on the foundation laid by Sanger. Does this mean that they are, knowingly or unknowingly, working for the cause of the power elite and helping to limit the number of "unfit" people?

Population Explosion and Lebensraum

The American eugenicists withdrew from the public eye during World War II because of the obvious espousing of eugenicist principles by the Nazis. After the war, many scientists abandoned the movement. This lasted less than a year and then Malthus's ideas were once again taken out of the closet, dusted off and combined with a new weapon: pollution. The reasoning was familiar: Because people pollute, an increase in the population will inevitably cause an increase in pollution.

This led to the expression "the population bomb" as part of an attempt to change the public image of the Population Bureau. In 1945 this institution published a monograph "Population, Roads to Peace and War." In 1947, Guy Irving Birch and Elmer Pendell revised it and published the book *Human Breeding and Survival.*. This book used the same reasoning— Lebensraum, (meaning *living space*)—that Hitler had used to justify his aggression against other nations. Only this time, it was combined with the eugenicist idea of the lower classes "outbreeding" the upper class. The power elite, therefore, needed more living space.

Other similar books were *Road to Survival,* by William Vote and *Our Plundered Planet,* by Fairfield Osborne. They were received very enthusiastically and led to the creation of the population movement.

All three books cited Malthus to put forth the prophecy that we would soon run out of resources and would, therefore, have to start following the laws of nature instead of exploiting them. Their version of the laws of nature included the old familiar ideas that the lower classes were less fit and should not be helped to survive; completely ignoring that it is actually an elite who is plundering the resources and polluting to maximize profits. These books recommended that no food be sent to Third World countries to keep the starving millions alive. Instead, the United States should set forth an example of how all civilized nations should deal with this inevitable result of population growth: Let them starve to death!

According to the books it was wrong that the medical profession was still following the ideals set forth by Hippocrates: to preserve life and keep as many people alive as possible. Helping people (from the lower classes, that is) to survive was only setting the stage for disaster. These three books were quickly turned into college text books and one of the students influenced by them in his freshman year was Paul Ehrlich.

Ehrlich's Population Bomb

In 1967, Paul Ehrlich published the book *The Population Bomb*. He used the thesis set forth in a book by the Paddock brothers called *Famine 1975* in which it was argued that all the poor nations simply could not survive. Because of this, the United States would be forced into a position of having to choose which nations should survive and which should not.

Ehrlich prophesied that hundreds of millions of people would die from starvation during the 1970s (as we can see, he wasn't a good prophet). He characterized the earth as a spaceship with a limited carrying capacity and said that population growth must stop. He even suggested the ideal size of the human crew. For the United States it was 150 million—so we now have about 100 million people that are simply excess baggage, according to Ehrlich.

Ehrlich said that it was absurd to worry about the medical quality of life (eradicating disease and saving lives), as long as we had not solved the problem of the quantity of life. He recommended that the government should apply chemicals causing sterilization to all food and water. Then, when people wanted children, they could apply to the government for an antidote. Of course, the government would have to come up with some kind of standard for how many children should be allowed to be born and who should be allowed to have them. Creating such a standard would have to involve the consideration of who is fit and who is not.

The curious thing about Ehrlich is that although he was a biologist, his specialty was insect populations. It should be obvious that the population dynamics in insect populations are quite different from the human population. A fly can lay thousands of eggs that hatch in a matter of days and the offspring can start laying eggs after a few weeks. A woman normally only bears one baby at a time and it takes 15 or so years before it can have children of its own. As several authors have pointed out, Ehrlich uncritically transferred the biological principles from insect to human populations.

Limits to Growth

The next step in the line of anti-population theories was a study done by the prestigious Club of Rome and published as a book entitled *Limits to Growth*. The study was an attempt to prove through a computer study that unless population and economic growth stopped on a planetary scale, we would all be doomed. The book became an instant best seller and had a tremendous impact in most Western nations where it was hailed as a revolutionary way to look at mankind. Regardless of all the nice words, the book and its conclusions are not true. The authors had less than one tenth of one percent of the data needed to construct a viable computer model. Furthermore, they only considered the behavior of "systems," completely disregarding how people in the real world behave. Under pressure, the authors finally admitted to the inaccuracies and admitted that the study was not objective but was made with a bias. What bias? Yes, our old friend Malthus. *Limits to Growth* was simply Malthus turned loose with a computer. The Club of Rome had to disavow the study, but they still held onto the conclusions—and so do millions of scientists, media people, bureaucrats and politicians today.

We have come full circle from Malthus in 1798 to the present. During all this time, the power elite has held onto Malthus's original theory, even though it has been disproven repeatedly by history. This is truly what Scott Peck refers to as "affirmation against all findings."

The irony of *The Population Bomb* and *Limits to Growth* is that both books were published in a time in which the population in the rich countries declined, food production increased tremendously and the standard of living was raised. As we already pointed out in the discussion of Malthus, the principle is unmistakable: When the standard of living is raised for the poor, population growth decreases. It is a fact that in many Third World countries having many children is a matter of survival. It is the only way for the parents to make sure that they can survive when they get too old to work. In nations where there is a social safety net, this motivation disappears and birth rates promptly drop.

The inescapable conclusion is that the best way to lower population growth is to raise the standard of living, which is quite in accordance with the Golden Rule expressed in the teachings of Christ and all major religions.

We have now reviewed how the theories about the population explosion have been developed and carried on over the centuries. It should be obvious that these theories have had a major impact on the abortion debate and have delivered much of the motivation behind the acceptance of abortion.

Is Overpopulation Real?

When we consider the number of uninhabited areas in the world and the resources not being used or being wasted, how can we claim that the planet is overpopulated? How can we say that the planet cannot sustain the number of people living on it right now? It is true that people in some nations are starving, but why are they starving? Is it because there is not enough food or is it because the available food is not distributed justly? Can't the land produce enough food? Or is the use of the land restricted by a power elite, preventing the people from using the resources efficiently? If people are dying from starvation, there are two options: A redistribution of wealth must occur or more wealth must be created (or both). In both cases, this will require a social change and this will often be prevented by a power elite holding on to their privileges. In how many Third World countries have we seen a power elite creating and maintaining a situation in which people are starving to death? How many times have we seen a power elite, as in Ethiopia, deliberately use mass starvation as a political and military weapon? And how many times have we seen our industrialized nations providing "humanitarian aid" without ever challenging the local power elite that created the problem in the first place?

We can see that "resource" is a relative concept. How many resources are available on this planet and how many people can this planet sustain if all resources are being used efficiently and distributed justly?

If we look at an agricultural society such as feudal Europe, there is a very tight limit to how big the population can be. It will be determined by how much food can be produced on the land that is available. Before we entered the technological age, there was a very narrow margin for how much grain could be grown on an acre of land. When all the arable land in a nation was being tilled, we had reached the upper limit for the size of the population. Technology changed this situation, because technology is essentially the process of doing more with less. In other words, through technology we have been able to expand the arable land (through irrigation, machinery, etc.) and we have been able to grow a much larger crop on an acre of land. This process is ongoing and who can tell when it will stop? With this in mind, how can we set a limit for the number of people this planet can feed? There may be limited amounts of certain resources, but there is no limit to creativity. Creativity is what allows us to look at a problem from a new perspective, come up with a higher understanding of reality and apply it as a new solution. Through creativity, we can expand the limitations of the past, as mankind has already done in numerous ways. Natural resources are not a finite thing. A good example is that 500 years ago oil was not seen as a natural resource. It was completely worthless because there was no knowledge of how to make practical use of it. Who can tell how a higher understanding can enable us to make use of substances we today see as worthless?

The only way mankind can ever run out of natural resources, food and wealth is if we run out of creativity. The only limitation is that certain people cannot see creativity as a solution to problems.

The Power Elite and
the Psychology of Limitation

Arnold Toynbee studied 26 civilizations of which 16 were dead and nine were broken down. On the basis of this study, he concluded that our civilization has entered a period of decay. He found that the inescapable lesson of history is that most civilizations self-destruct.

According to Toynbee, the survival of a civilization depends on its leaders. The outcome depends on whether the creative or the dominant minority is in command. The dominant minority are the people Fromm called necrophiliacs and he also said they are people who are seeking to gain personal power by controlling everything. They want to maintain status quo by making everything predictable. Necrophiliacs have no creative flow, they are completely ego-centered and they cannot see creativity as a solution to any problem. That is why they are striving to organize a society that is not dependent on creativity, an unpredictable phenomenon, but rather one in which everything can be foreseen. I believe it is very important for us to recognize that necrophiliacs will work actively against changes in society even if it means suppressing new, creative solutions. This could explain why new inventions are sometimes suppressed by influential people. For example, some European aristocrats opposed the building of railroads because it would allow the lower classes to move around needlessly.

The essence of the power elite syndrome is a sense of limitation which springs from a fear of loss. It is a belief that there is only a certain amount of food, natural resources and wealth available on this planet. It follows that when the population grows, there will be more people to share the same amount. If a small elite has managed to get hold of most of the wealth, a growing population will necessarily have to take something from the elite. To the power elite, there is only one way to go and that is down. They believe they can only lose and to prevent this loss they seek to prevent change.

What we have to realize is that this kind of reasoning is the result of a necrophilic consciousness, a consciousness that has lost touch with principles and become polarized to the human ego. I think we should seriously question the paradigm that life on this planet is governed by a set of very narrow limitations. I believe it is quite possible that, through creativity, we can push our limits and gain a new level of material as well as spiritual freedom.

The Savior With a Time Machine

According to Toynbee, the dominant minority creates a number of seemingly unsolvable problems that will put society in a gridlock. The only way to overcome this situation is that society must transcend itself by looking beyond the official paradigms. I believe Toynbee would agree that the problem is that society has become too ego-centered and that the only way out is to get back to timeless principles. As an interesting footnote I would like to mention that Toynbee also concluded that the only road to survival for any civilization is the adoption of a universal religion. I have attempted to point to a synthesis between religion and science as the possible origin for such a universal faith.

The dominant minority are unable to return to principles, so according to Toynbee they will seek to appear as the savior with a time machine. Since they are out of touch with the creative nature of life itself, they are always behind evolution seeking to stop it instead of flowing with it. They want to bring society backwards into the state it was in earlier, that is, a state of control by a power elite that has now been overrun by the forward movement of life.

The feudal society of medieval Europe was overrun by the forward movement of time, but the power elite of today seeks to bring us back to a society with centralized control and monopolized privileges. Today, they do it with the means available to them and they use whatever ideas appear persuasive to the people of our time.

In all reality, the power elite is fighting for an impossible cause, because it is not possible to stop the forward movement of life. Yet, they are trying to create a society in which this has supposedly been accomplished, and they believe they can do this through control. To control everything, you must be able to predict everything and the very nature of creativity is that it cannot be predicted. The essence of the creative process is that you take known elements and combine them, bringing about an entirely new phenomenon.

The power elite is trying to accomplish their ends by making the people accept that the unexpected is automatically the same as the unwanted. Therefore, we must stop all activities for which we cannot predict the outcome, stop all creativity and set up a mechanized society. Any new technological invention is automatically seen as a threat. An unexpected pregnancy is automatically an unwanted pregnancy. Therefore, in the name of giving people freedom from the unexpected, we must control everything. This is turning things completely around by saying that freedom can only be found in total control. On the contrary, control leads to the loss of freedom, because true freedom is transcendence of limitations and the very heart of the creative process.

It is a major problem that the majority of the population cannot understand the way the dominant minority thinks and they are often defenseless against their attempts to take over. Most people cannot imagine that there could be a minority seeking to manipulate our society away from the evolution of life itself so that they can gain absolute control. They find it hard to believe that what we see as absolute limitations to the growth of our civilization is simply a fantasy, the product of sick minds. But how else can we explain that so many of these so-called limitations are the result of a flawed reasoning?

We have already noted that the idea of overpopulation is the result of a flawed reasoning. Some sociologists have predicted that within the next 50 years the world population will stabilize at around 10 billion people. Can the planet sustain 10 billion people? Who can say? What we can say, however, is that it cannot sustain 10 billion people with the present amount and distribution of wealth. Again, we face the two options of creating more wealth and creating a more just distribution. The big question is, will we solve this problem through control or through creativity?

The entire environmental debate today is focused on the need for creating centralized control with the use of natural resources. Many environmentalists are supporting abortion because they accept the idea that the cause of our environmental problems is the growing population. Most environmentalists want to put the state in control of all use of natural resources, which is the same type of society as in feudal Europe. The environmental issue is rapidly becoming one of the most powerful political factors in all the democratic nations. Unfortunately, most people have not yet realized that it too can be used to undermine freedom and democracy.

The question we need to ask is whether the problem is people or just certain people? Who is creating the problems our society is facing, the general population or the power elite?

Let us end by mentioning that technology may not be able to solve all the problems we are facing, but what is technology? In its essence, technology is the practical outcome of the principle Alexander applied when he took care of the Gordian knot. What he did was to look at the problem from a new perspective. He dared to look beyond the boundaries set up by orthodox thinking. By looking at the problems from a new perspective, we can get a higher understanding of our situation. Our civilization may have hit upon certain outer limitations. There is only so much land to discover and we may already have discovered most of it. The limitations we see for our civilization are all material, physical and outer limitations. We know we have not even begun to understand all there is to know about life. If we begin to look for a higher understanding, a new approach to life, who can tell what avenues can open up? Instead of accepting the boundaries of the material world as limitations for the growth of our civilization, we need to look beyond. We need to realize that there are worlds beyond the physical universe that we have evidence of, but which we do not yet understand.

We have been through the French Revolution, the American Revolution, the technological revolution, and the agricultural revolution. How about bringing about a revolution in consciousness, seeking to transcend the limitations that we, with the help of a few necrophiliacs, have set up in our own minds?

The eternal fact of human life is that we will never know what lies beneath the horizon of our conscious minds until we dare go see for ourselves. The eternal fact of social life is that any change in a society begins with one individual: You.

CHAPTER 12

What Brings About Change in Society?

I was brought up with what I now believe is a slightly naive idea of how democracies came into being. This paradigm stated that modern democracies resulted from a universal drive to create a society with freedom and liberty for all, and that everyone agrees with this drive. If this was true, then here are a few questions we might ask. Why has it often taken violence and bloodshed to establish democratic nations? Why aren't all nations democracies? Why has it taken thousands of years to bring forth democracies? After all, they have only been in existence for a little over two hundred years. Why are the "old" democracies becoming more and more centralized, with the governments assuming still more power over the people? Why don't we have justice and liberty as a practical reality in our democracies?

What was it that forced the kings and the noble class of feudal Europe to give way to democracy? The answer is simple: Scientific discoveries, technological inventions and a growing population. These factors are, of course, intertwined, but let us concentrate on the growing population.

In medieval Europe the economy was centralized, with a small power elite having almost total control. The economy was monopolized with a very uneven distribution of wealth and economic opportunity. The available food supply could only sustain a certain number of "common" people. Knowledge about disease, better hygiene and a number of other factors caused the population to grow, creating tension with the power elite. When the population reached a certain level, the poor majority of the people could no longer survive—not because there wasn't enough food, but because it was not distributed justly.

Until this time, the population had been so suppressed that they had neither the knowledge, nor the drive to revolt against the established powers. When people are facing death from starvation, it becomes very difficult for an elite to suppress them. Because the power elite refused to change society voluntarily, the tension eventually became so great that a violent confrontation occurred. The catalyst that broke the status quo was the growing population. If the elite had been able to keep the population at the level where people could survive with the existing distribution of wealth, democracies still might not be in existence.

The United States might not exist either because it was the growing population of Europe that led to its colonization. When the population grows beyond the boundaries set by the elite, people must either fight or flee or both.

How Individuals Produce Change in Society

Another way in which people bring about change is through individual initiative and creativity. In many instances, one person has produced major change in society. One unique individual can cause a change by formulating a new philosophy or idea, making a new invention or discovery, or by acting as the leader to free the people from the bondage of an established power elite. Some prime examples are Abraham, Moses, Jesus, Columbus, Galileo, Newton, George Washington, Abraham Lincoln, Einstein, Madame Curie and Gandhi.

When progress happens, it is often because one individual inspires the general population to look beyond the relative human consciousness and take a stand for a new and higher understanding. We could almost define this as a universal principle, in which one person is the catalyst that causes a chain reaction, producing a dramatic shift in consciousness. What we might ask is, could this change have been brought about by any other person than the one doing it? Could "anybody" have replaced one of the great persons of history?

From the standpoint of the power elite, the reaction to this "problem" is quite simple. As Scott Peck seeks to demonstrate in his book, these people do not reason the way normal people do. They do not consider right and wrong according to any superior standard or principle. They follow an "ends-justifies-the-means" attitude because to them the discussion of right or wrong is irrelevant. They do not consider whether something is right or wrong if it can produce the result they desire, which in this case is to prevent a change that will threaten their position. They will, without giving it a second thought, sacrifice others to acquire or maintain privileges. They simply conclude that when an individual becomes a threat, he must be eliminated. The power elite threatened or killed many of the great men and women of history. Often these people were killed before their mission was completed, causing it to fail, and preventing a positive change in society.

Our present civilization could be seen as one step in a process directed towards ending human suffering. The means for doing this are many: There are new ideas in religion and philosophy; there are new discoveries in the fields of science, medicine and technology; there are new political thoughts and refinements of our moral and ethical standards. Each of these stepping stones of progress is brought into the world by people. Often it is one specific person who possesses the genius necessary to do what no one else has been able to do thus far. That person has the capacity to look beyond the established positions and find a new perspective. Sometimes it is one person alone who brings forth the idea, and sometimes there is a succession of people, each one building upon the discoveries of his predecessors. One might get the idea that for every problem facing mankind there is one specific individual, or group of individuals, with the key to the solution.

Since Roe v. Wade, 25 million abortions have been performed in the United States alone and many millions more worldwide. Some people proclaim it is only fetal tissue that was aborted, but the fact remains that if these abortions had not taken place, there would have been almost 25 million more people alive today in the United States alone. We might ask ourselves what kind of individuals they would have been? What would have been their unique contribution to our society and the progression of our civilization? We can be sure that out of 25 million people there would have been some scientists, philosophers, doctors, inventors and politicians. Were there some among them that could have given a unique contribution to the quest for ending human suffering such as a cure for cancer? Perhaps someone who could have caused a dramatic change in society? Have we, by aborting these 25 million potential persons, aborted the solution to one of the major problems facing mankind? We will never know, but if we want to have a full perspective on abortion, such speculations must be part of it.

It has always surprised me that no one has yet done a study of the sociological consequences of abortion. Modern sociologists have developed a number of sophisticated methods for predicting changes in a population. I think these tools should be put to use in answering the question of what our society would have looked like today if no abortions had been performed over the past two decades.

Changing Times

There has been a flood of Christian and New Age books on the market in recent decades addressing major world changes that could come in the last decade of this century. Perhaps a majority of the population believe we are on the threshold of a major change on the world scene.

Many Christian denominations believe in concepts such as the Battle of Armageddon, in which forces of light will ultimately defeat forces of darkness. Many Christians also believe in a Second Coming, in which Christ will once more appear in this world. There are several different versions of these beliefs. The common element in them is that we are on the verge of seeing a major world transformation whereby the powers of this world lose the battle with those from a higher world. This higher world is essentially what we earlier referred to as the "absolute level of existence." Another approach is held by people belonging to what is referred to as "new age" groups. As the name implies, they also have a common belief in a new and better age. The different versions of these ideas are as varied as the many Christian doctrines, but again there is a clear belief in major world change.

Let us consider how this new and better age could come about. There are many possibilities, but we cannot deny that people will play a major role in all of them. Even if we consider Jesus to be above and beyond normal human beings, his mission still depended upon ordinary people. Jesus needed his disciples, apostles and the many people in the "inner circle" around him to complete his mission. If no one had responded to his words, the Christian faith would not have survived. Today, just as in the time of Jesus, world change will involve people. If these people are not alive because they have been aborted, how will this influence potential world change?

We must consider the importance of the individual. Perhaps certain individuals are necessary to cause this coming world change. Maybe they have the unique individuality that gives them the keys to creating a society with less human suffering. How many of these individuals would statistically have been among the 25 million people aborted since 1973?

If we believe the world is approaching a major change, and this change will bring about a better society, we must assume that our present society is less than ideal. Obviously, there is much suffering and a lack of freedom, but what is the cause? Could the existence of one or several power elite groups seeking to control the population have anything to do with it? Is the reason we do not have a better society that progress has been held back or obstructed? Has it been blocked by the actions of a power elite determined to maintain privileges taken from the general population? We can hardly deny that such privileges exist, since we all realize there is injustice and discrimination in our society.

The new world many of us dream about would not be the ideal playground for power elites. The very nature of our dream is a world with more freedom, justice and abundance for everyone. Perhaps this coming new world means a world in which there is no power elite, a society in which the people cannot be dominated and ruled by earthly powers? Maybe the people are finally going to rise up and overthrow the power elites of this world. Again, certain individuals will be the key.

Many people, in religious and new-age groups alike, believe that there are forces from higher levels seeking to work with humanity to bring about this change. They say these higher beings of light need "ordinary people" to work through one way or the other and might depend on specific individuals to perform certain tasks. It's possible that these forces are actively seeking to bring individual lifestreams into the world and place them in the position that will give them the best circumstances for performing their mission. We must admit, if such an effort exists, abortion could wreak havoc and either delay or destroy the efforts to produce change. When will we have reached the critical point in which so many of these specific individuals have been aborted that it is no longer possible to bring about a new age? Is it possible that we are aborting a new and better world?

CHAPTER 13

True and False Rights

What Is Freedom?

The abortion debate has given much attention to the pregnant woman and her freedom of choice. I think it is reasonable that we take a closer look at what freedom really is. Is it freedom when you can do whatever you want? Not necessarily, because every human action has some kind of aftermath. If we do what we want today without considering the consequences, these consequences may restrict our freedom tomorrow. Everyday experience tells us that when considering what freedom is, we should think in longer terms than the present. Yet in our society we are programmed to do what we want now, without thinking about the results. It is like a merchant saying, "Sign this contract now and I will tell you the price later." If you don't know the full consequences, or if you ignore them, how can you make a free choice?

We can ask another question: "Is it true that our democratic society should guarantee our freedom, and if so, what kind of freedom does it guarantee?" Again, we could say that there is true freedom and false freedom. False freedom will give us short-term options, but it restricts our choices in the long run. The true freedom may seem like a restriction now, but it will protect our future freedom. If a democratic society is to guarantee freedom, it must strive to preserve true freedom.

But what is true freedom? It is a freedom that is not dependent on any factors in the relative world of time and space. In other words, true freedom must be based on and defined by timeless principles. Only freedom that is not given by or dependent upon, any earthly authority or power can be said to be true freedom. The anything-goes attitude, which is the brainchild of the human ego, is in total opposition to democratic principles and can only destroy a democracy. Anarchy is not freedom. It is simply another form of slavery in which the individual has become subject to relative forces, either in his surroundings or in his own psychology.

In short, true freedom is not the lack of any kind of restrictions. True freedom is to act within the framework of principles so that we do not work up a debt to life that we do not want to repay.

By now we can ask: If we have the correct understanding of freedom, and if our definition of freedom incorporates inalienable rights, can there ever be a conflict between one freedom and another? Can there ever be a conflict between inalienable rights if these rights are understood correctly?

The abortion debate seems to be a clash between the freedom of the unborn to live and the freedom of the woman to choose. Is this conflict the result of a lack in our understanding of freedom? A way to answer this question is to look at how nature works.

We have hinted that there are different levels of existence, such as the relative level and a higher level that we call the absolute level. But even on the relative level of existence, there are different levels or layers. In the animal kingdom, there is a variety of life forms, ranging from what we call primitive to more sophisticated. The same with many other parts of nature. Life seems to progress in stages from uncomplicated (general) to more sophisticated (specific) levels. The more sophisticated life forms have a greater freedom to act; they have more options. Should we consider if there are levels of freedom and inalienable rights?

The Declaration of Independence states that all men have the inalienable right to life, liberty, and the pursuit of happiness. Is the sequence of these words chosen randomly, or does it reflect a progression? What is the most basic of these three rights? Obviously, the right to life, because if you don't have life, how can you have freedom or pursue happiness? The second most basic right is liberty; for without it you cannot choose how to pursue your happiness. Hence, the right to life is really the foundation for any other right we can define.

First things first, which means there are at least three levels on which we can define rights.

The most fundamental level is where we find the right to life. On the next level, we find the right to liberty, or freedom of choice, for all who have life. The third level is the right to pursue happiness as one sees fit, but still within the framework of eternal values.

We might argue whether the right to privacy belongs on the second or third level, but there is no doubt that it cannot be placed on the first level. In other words, the most fundamental right, the right to life, cannot clash with or be neutralized by a less fundamental (more specific) right.

Why does the abortion debate appear to be a clash of absolutes between the right to life and the right to liberty? Is it because our ethical or moral understanding is too primitive, or because we do not yet understand what true freedom is?

Ego-centered and Principle-centered Rights

By accepting the idea described in Part 2 about a spiritual side to life; we can take our concerns for the pregnant woman one step further. We must concern ourselves about her spiritual growth as the very foundation for her liberty and happiness. Now that she is facing an unplanned pregnancy, our question should be, "How can we help her resolve this situation in a way that will not limit her spiritual growth and thereby destroy her chances of finding true happiness?"

So far, the abortion debate has been dominated by two forces. The pro-life faction essentially says: The unborn child has a right to life which is more fundamental than the mother's right to choose. If she believes having a child will limit her pursuit of happiness, then that is simply a fact of life she will have to live with. The pro-choice faction says: We have a fundamental right to choose and if an unplanned pregnancy will limit a woman's happiness, she has the right to end it without considering any consequences.

The reason for this division might be that both the right to life and the right to freedom of choice are very important to us. They are both fundamental to the philosophical basis of a democratic society. One of the men involved with creating

America, Patrick Henry, said, "Give me liberty or give me death," stating that if he did not have freedom to make his own choices, he would prefer not to be alive. Many of us can identify with this feeling because life and freedom are inseparable. What is the purpose of being alive if you do not have freedom, which essentially means freedom to grow spiritually.

The most unfortunate result of the abortion debate is that a great number of people have come to see these two rights as being in opposition to each other. Since both sides believe they are defending a fundamental right, neither of them is willing to bend and the tension keeps growing. The only way to resolve this conflict is to seek a higher understanding and perhaps the perspective that life has a spiritual side could provide it.

If we accept that the purpose of life is spiritual growth and that man has been given free will, we must assume that making choices is an inseparable part of our spiritual development. It is by seeing the consequences of our choices that we gain an opportunity to expand our understanding of "the mechanics of life" and adjust our attitude and opinions accordingly. Thus we could say that our free will is the very basis for this growth. Only when we have complete freedom of choice do we have the maximum opportunity for developing spiritually. We must, however, acknowledge that it is one thing to have a right, but another to be in a position to exercise it. In many countries, people are not able to speak their minds because their governments would persecute them for it. A recent poll found that two-thirds of U. S. high school students believe rights are defined by the government. Nevertheless, the majority of Americans would probably agree that people in a totalitarian country still have the right of freedom of speech. They are just not in a position to exercise it.

When it comes to freedom of choice, outer factors will, of course, have an influence on how we can exercise that right. But freedom of choice really begins inside ourselves. We cannot choose freely unless we know all of our options and their consequences. If we do not have the full understanding of the situation in which we have to choose, we are really not in a position to exercise our right of freedom of choice! Doing whatever we feel like in our immediate situation and with our present knowledge is not a right. We could even call it a false right, because it is based on a false choice. We must acknowledge that we do not have a right to make uninformed choices, neither do we have a right to willfully ignore information that is available.

Our society acknowledges that people have a right to smoke. When the medical profession first began to prove a link between smoking and cancer, the tobacco industry would much have preferred that people had remained ignorant about this. Yet the government decided that people did not have the right to smoke without knowing that they would increase their risk of cancer. We have a right to choose, but only when it is an informed choice.

People have a right to drive a car and they have a right to drink alcohol. But they do not have a right to drive a car while being intoxicated because they are likely to hurt themselves or others. Suicide is prohibited by law, because we know that most suicides take place when people are in an unbalanced frame of mind. We do not have a right to make choices that are clearly self-destructive. Although some say that ignorance is bliss, we do not have a right to be stupid and this is written into our laws!

We must also consider the idea of a true and a false freedom that we described earlier. Doing whatever we want without seeing any personal accountability is a false freedom. True freedom is to express our individuality within the framework of natural law. Ignoring or willfully disobeying natural law is not a right, and a democratic government has no obligation to protect such a false right.

It is curious to note that individuals, as well as governments, will sometimes apply one set of rules to one situation and another set to another situation. Right now the American government will not allow people to smoke without knowing that it can cause cancer, but they do uphold a woman's right to make an uninformed choice concerning abortion.

If we acknowledge the idea that life has a spiritual side, then we must consider the idea of spiritual consequences. We can all observe that our physical actions in most cases have some kind of physical outcomes. Before we make a decision to act, we routinely and often subconsciously, evaluate the possible consequences. We do this to see if the price we might have to pay is worth the potential benefit of our actions. As we have seen earlier, we live in a culture in which much teaching about the spiritual side of life has been deliberately suppressed by different power elites at different times. The result is that most people are not even aware of the idea that their actions could have spiritual consequences. They simply do not have the perspective that their actions in this life could affect them even after they have died. Or rather, that their actions could affect the spiritual self, the soul, after the death of the physical body. Without this view, how can we have a full understanding of our options and their effects? How can we be in a position to exercise our right to make an informed choice? Can we say that a woman has freedom of choice concerning abortion when she has no knowledge of the potential spiritual consequences of her choice? As long as such a spiritual understanding is not commonplace, we could raise the question if the right to chose an abortion is a true or a false right? Is our government in all reality upholding a false right which causes women to make a choice they would not have made if they had known there were effects beyond the physical? Does a woman have a right to limit the growth of her own higher self? And would she choose to do so if she knew what was at stake?

Most of the suppression of spiritual knowledge took place in earlier societies with more totalitarian governments. Yet, our present government has done nothing to correct the repression enacted by these earlier powers, and we might ask why? We know that the early suppression was caused by a power elite that did not want the people to gain full spiritual understanding, because it would set them free from domination by worldly powers. Is our present government still acting as a tool for such a power elite, or is it simply as much a victim of the early repression as the rest of us? If the latter is the case, one might look for a willingness to correct the problem by opening up the institutions of government to a debate about spiritual values.

The abortion debate has clearly polarized our society and it is forcing us all to take a stand, to make a choice. However, the choice we must make is not a simple matter of being pro-choice or pro-life. It is much more profound and it goes to the very heart of our beings. In all reality, we are being forced to choose between two completely opposite approaches to life.

Our first option is to grow. We can use the lack of resolution in the abortion debate to reason that we are lacking in our spiritual understanding of life. We can then redirect our efforts, both on an individual and an organizational level, to seek for such a spiritual renewal. We can choose to look beyond our present positions to seek truth wherever it can be found. This is the choice of a lifetime, because we will then seek to fulfill our inner soul desire for spiritual growth. Such a choice has the potential for not only resolving the abortion issue, but for bringing a much needed spiritual renewal into our society and a new sense of fulfillment into our lives.

Our second option is to choose to ignore the need for this development. We can refuse to consider the spiritual aspects of the abortion issue and continue to approach the conflict through material means. Making this choice is to accept stagnation and ultimately it is to side with death. The outcome of this choice is rather predictable. Just as it happened with the Civil War, tension will continue to grow and the inevitable result will be large scale violence.

How can we overcome our cultural lack of spiritual insight, and where can we find a more comprehensive teaching on spiritual matters than we have in the high school curriculum? There is an enormous body of so-called esoteric or mystical teachings available, both in the Christian tradition, in other religions and philosophies. In fact, if we dared take a look beyond the traditional approach that only one religion can be right and therefore all others must be false, we could quickly assemble a vast body of knowledge bridging the gap between orthodox religions. By comparing this body of knowledge to the latest discoveries of modern science, I think it would be possible to piece together a new spiritual world view. This new paradigm could be made so universal that it would not exclude existing religions or churches; it would merely expand them. It could possibly create a common ground that would allow people from all religious and non-religious backgrounds to realize that we all have something in common. Behind all the surface appearances, we are all souls that are traveling on the same path towards a deeper understanding of the mysteries of life.

Such a new development would require a willingness to seek truth wherever it could be found, regardless of our outer preferences or preconceptions. On the basis of an observation of history, it can be predicted that such a spiritual renewal is not likely to come from the government or the major media, since it will require us to go beyond the doctrines of the established powers in both church and state. It will, as most of the spiritual renewals of the past, have to come from beneath, from the people, through a grassroots effort.

CHAPTER 14

Sex and Society

We Live and Breathe Sex

Most of the women seeking an abortion belong to the younger generation. There seems to be a growing number of unplanned pregnancies among young women, even teenagers. I think this is illogical. The younger generation today has received a more comprehensive sex education than any generation in this century. Hardly anyone can fail to know what causes a pregnancy or know the practical measures for avoiding a pregnancy. Why then are a growing number of young women getting pregnant?

We know that even when established couples use contraceptive measures, a certain percentage of unplanned pregnancies occurs. We can assume that the more sex people have, the more pregnancies will occur, and this might be the answer why. Most people will agree that young people of today generally have more sex and generally start earlier than people of a generation or two ago. We might ask why?

An obvious answer is that young people of today must have a different attitude to sex than young people of a generation or so ago. What caused this change?

Let us start with the realization that there is a battle going on in the minds of mankind between the traditional Christian and the modern scientific perspectives. The Christian attitude towards sex was, and is in general, very restrictive. This attitude has an element of guilt in it, since it is assumed that sex was what caused Adam and Eve to be cast out of Paradise. Since this attitude to sex was not accompanied by any spiritual understanding, many people began to see it as a restriction of their freedom.

Today many people refuse to feel guilty about sex which is probably a very healthy reaction. As a result they are looking for a different perspective. This was delivered through the scientific belief system in which sex is seen simply as a biological function. It was the intellectual elite that first began to disassociate sex from the traditional value system. Sex outside marriage, more sex and sex with different partners became quite common among this self-appointed elite after the turn of the century. The general population of that time was reluctant to follow suit, because for most people, sex was a very private matter. They didn't want to have it portrayed as a mere biological function; once again a very healthy reaction. So, it took a long time to change the general population's attitude to sex (many people still refuse to see sex as a mere biological function), and the breakthrough didn't occur until the 60's. That was when the so-called sexual revolution occurred in which mankind was supposedly freed from all "unnatural" restrictions relating to sex. What caused this revolution? Let us look at two factors: education and the media.

Education and Sex

The battle between the Christian and scientific paradigms was fought with great vigor in the field of education. In the 60s, the people promoting the scientific approach finally seemed to have broken down the Christian's last stand and the result was sex education.

In many Western nations, children were exposed to sex education as early as the age of 12. Although a few may have some interest at that age, the majority merely have a sense of curiosity, not the emotional maturity to deal with the subject directly. However, sex education forces children to deal with the subject in a very direct way and generally gives a very one-sided presentation of the issue.

There are a variety of emotions related to the relationship between the two sexes and there is obviously more to it than physical interaction. Most modern sex education only deals with the "mechanics" of the physical act, describing it in a factual, scientific way. Many children (although they would probably not be able to formulate it) end up with a very unbalanced view of the issue. They are taught in school that sex is something we can study and relate to in an "objective" manner as if there were no feelings involved. Yet, they clearly experience a variety of very strong emotions in themselves, but they receive no help in handling these emotions. The result is a conflict and many children resolve it in a very distinct way.

When a human being is faced with emotions that are too strong to handle, a very common reaction is withdrawal. Young teenagers often withdraw emotionally from the issue of sex and thereby they withdraw from the spiritual aspects of not only sex, but their entire relationship to the opposite sex. Interaction with the opposite sex is reduced to a physical act, a mere biological function. Is that why so many people in the younger generations have more sex and with many different partners? If sex is a physical act, a biological function, then, it follows that no moral or ethical aspects apply—anything goes. Unfortunately, this attitude completely ignores the issue of the very delicate and tender feeling called love.

A growing number of adults who were teenagers in the 60s are beginning to realize that the sexual revolution actually did not bring them any freedom. Many people who have lived the "freedom" of the sexual revolution admit, at least to themselves, that it was a big failure. It did not give freedom, it merely catapulted people from one extreme (the too restrictive Christian attitude) to the other extreme (the excessively permissive scientific attitude). What was won in terms of physical freedom was lost in an emotional and spiritual tyranny. The so-called sexual freedom has caused many people to feel empty inside, to feel emotionally raped. It is as if an excessive sexual activity causes people to lose vital energy, making them feel spiritually empty. Ironically, this was all done in the name of freedom.

The Media and Sex

During the 60s, most of the media in the western world went through a gradual transformation and began dealing with sex more directly. In pictures and writing, sex was displayed freely. Sex was portrayed as a physical act disassociated from any delicate feelings. It was linked to raw power and unmasked physical desire with little respect for the more tender aspects of life.

A picture may say more than a thousand words, but pictures are not very suited for communicating the more tender feelings. The display of sex in pictures tends to make most people withdraw emotionally.

Another important factor is the value system that became associated with sex. It is true that earlier sex had been associated with a sense of guilt that is no doubt unhealthy. But many of the restrictions related to sex and its display in public stem from the fact that for most people sex is a very private matter. They don't want it to be displayed openly because it is a violation of the feelings involved. The media completely ignored these emotions and began portraying sex openly as if it was very much undesirable to hide the subject in the bedroom. Hereby, many adults withdrew emotionally just as school children had done in sex education class. Because of this withdrawal, people quickly became numbed to the display of sex.

At the same time, the entire advertising industry picked up the trend and started a very deliberate use of sex as a sales tool. Images that somehow triggered a sexual stimulus were used in advertising and still are. Today we are surrounded by images related to sex; it is even used in seemingly innocent commercials. We live and breathe sex!

What happened during the 60s was that our society was triggered into focusing on sex as not only the most important, but almost as the only way for the two sexes to interact. Out of the entire cornucopia of interactions between the sexes, the media focused on one single factor, the physical act of sex. This act was disassociated from any delicate feelings and this "nonemotional" form of sex was then portrayed as a new freedom.

It is an irony that much of the drive behind the sexual revolution was delivered by women in the name of women's liberation. By disassociating sex from deeper feelings, women during the 60s finally became reduced to what they were seeking to escape—being mere physical objects for sexual exploitation. Now a man needed to have no sense of responsibility for a woman. He could have sex with her and did not have to consider if she had any feelings involved with the process. If she happened to become pregnant, then he had no need to feel accountable because the solution was so simple, she could just have an abortion. And, of course, the issue of abortion was likewise disassociated from any deeper emotions. Some pro-choice activists never talk about the emotional reaction of women having an abortion, they seem to see it as a mere biological occurrence with no feelings involved.

What is really happening is that people have become reduced to biological functions, to an animal level or even a robot—with no deeper feelings at all. In the educational systems, the media and many other institutions of our society, people are being treated as objects. The subject of human emotions is completely ignored.

Yet, emotions are one of the fundamental factors separating man from animals. If a person's feelings become numbed, he or she is, in a sense, functioning like an animal. Some genetic engineers are seriously contemplating the creation of a new type of being that could function as a slave race to do all the hard work—a living robot with human capabilities but without that problematic factor: human emotions. In a sense, this idea of a slave race with no emotions has always been the dream of the power elite. Have they been trying to turn the rest of us into robots with no feelings by seeking to program us through social engineering?

What we might consider is that sex is not simply a physical act done for the sake of getting a temporary pleasure; it is the very process by which life begets new life. Therefore, sex is fundamental to the survival of the race. We can safely assume that there are a variety of very deep emotions associated with such a basic process. Is it in our own best interest to ignore these emotions?

The Exploitation of Women

In Part One we noted the necessity to look for ego-centered motives so, as a thought-experiment, let us try to imagine how a manipulator could use the abortion debate for political purposes. Since deception is the way to manipulate people in a democracy, we could imagine that a manipulator would seek to appear as the beneficiary of one group of people while in reality using this group in a hidden agenda. We can therefore, deduct a principle for how manipulators could work: They seek out a target group within the population and appear to work for the freedom of the target group. In reality, they are using the target group as a lever to force a change upon society. It follows that the key to success is to make the right choice of the target group. How would a manipulator choose his target group? By finding out which group is the most vulnerable and therefore the easiest to manipulate!

Which kind of people are the most vulnerable in this context? Obviously the woman who has just realized that she is facing an unexpected or unplanned pregnancy. She is facing a set of very severe, and for most women, frightening circumstances. Her body is going to change in a way that is disturbing and often frightening. If the pregnancy is the result of a one-time sexual affair (which she has been encouraged to have as part of her liberation as a woman), she knows she can expect no support whatsoever from the child's father. If she has a steady relationship with the father, she is facing a possible breakup or, at the very least, a serious change in their relationship. She is most likely facing a disruption of her lifestyle, education or career. She is facing a likely condemnation from her friends, her society and her own family. She may be facing financial difficulties that can easily seem like a major threat to her future lifestyle.

All in all, such a woman is in a position where she can easily be brought into a state of mind that makes it very difficult for her to think ahead and consider long-term perspectives. A woman who has just found out she is pregnant and who has had no time to consider the situation, or to seek the advice of others, is the perfect target group for someone who is out to prevent pregnancies that lead to babies.

The first step in manipulation is to set up the smoke screen. This is done by declaring that these women should have the freedom to choose their own destiny. The freedom of the pregnant woman is defined as being more important than the freedom of the unborn child. The freedom to choose is defined as a right, even as a constitutional right, that can replace the unborn child's right to life. The right of the woman to choose freely is defined as more important than the right of the unborn child to get into a situation where he or she can start making choices.

To ensure the success of such an idea, two things must happen:

1. A situation must be set up that propels the target

group into a state of desperation and then offers them an easy way out. This is done by establishing counseling centers that offer women a free pregnancy test and then present the problems relating to pregnancy and childrearing without touching upon alternatives. When the woman has been brought into a state of desperation, she is then offered the easy way out: an abortion.

2. Other groups of people must support the idea. This can be done by making some people believe in the idea and the benefits of the idea, and by making sure certain people will gain a personal advantage from supporting the idea.

Abortion is the perfect issue for a manipulation because it does bring up some very real problems. The horrors of back-alley abortions are real. Many women have been forced into poverty or other unfortunate circumstances by unplanned pregnancies. In other words, there are a lot of victims of these problems who are looking for a solution. It is, therefore, almost inevitable that there will be a number of sincere, honest and goodhearted people, willing to support an idea that seems to put an end to these very real and valid problems. What these people do not realize is that the abortion solution may not be based entirely on unselfish motives.

When a woman can easily escape an unplanned pregnancy through abortion, it will not be necessary to enact social changes that could make it easier for her to raise a child without facing poverty. Hereby we avoid social upheaval that could pose a threat to the privileges of the established elite. In a way the well-meaning people supporting such a false idea become another target group for the power elite.

It has always surprised me that neither of the two sides in the debate are talking more about how society could make it easier for women to support their children. It seems reasonable that a woman can hold a job or pursue a career while having children. If a lot of women, as some polls seem to show, would like to have children, but feel it would be too difficult, then abortion seems like a cheap way out.

The best way to make people support a certain idea is to give them a chance to gain a personal benefit from it. When freedom of choice entered the public debate, one of the first organized groups to support it was the women's liberation movement. Since then, this movement has gained more political recognition and support than ever before. Is this merely coincidence or is it because the liberation movement gained a political advantage from supporting the goals of a manipulator?

Since the idea of freedom of choice began to gain popular support, many politicians have jumped on the bandwagon. For some of them it was the one thing that got them elected—most politician's main concern. Some people are driven by a desire for personal power and these political animals support just about any cause they believe can get them elected. Even sincere and honest politicians can be tempted to espouse a popular cause since a politician who is not elected will have very little influence. So, a manipulator can use these people's desire to get elected as a lever to get support for their idea.

Finally we have to consider the question of dollars. The medical profession has to some degree been influenced by the god of mammon. It is a fact that many doctors, medical professionals and counselors have attained quite impressive personal incomes by providing services relating to abortion on demand. A manipulator would be well aware that some people can be bought, either by position or by money.

The idea of a woman's right to freedom of choice has, so far, led to a situation in which the political establishment has affirmed her right to have an abortion on demand. Furthermore, it has been established that a minor does not have to ask or even inform her parents. No woman has to ask or inform the child's father, even if he has been her husband for 20 years. Right now, no woman is required to obtain information about fetal development in the womb, about the dangers and possible side effects of abortion or about alternatives such as adoption.

It seems as if everything that can be done has been done to ensure that a woman has complete freedom to choose an abortion and that no one can influence her choice. That is, no one who might prevent her choice of an abortion.

What are the real motives behind the talk about freedom of choice? If we are truly concerned about the woman as an individual human being, we should be enflamed by a desire to see her make the best possible decision, a decision she will never regret.

Can we truly say that our society is defending a woman's freedom and her right to make a fully informed choice? Does the woman have a free choice or has somebody tried to make the choice for her? Are women really benefiting from our present legislation about abortion? If not, who is gaining an advantage from the situation? There are only two options. Either the entire situation is the result of a manipulation by a power elite, or it is the result of a debate that went awry without anyone understanding why. In either case, every sincere person should have a strong desire to see some real changes, especially every woman who is a victim of the present situation. Whether women are the victims of a conscious manipulation or of plain ignorance, they are still victims. If we let go of the paradigm that our present version of freedom of choice is in the best interest of women, it might allow us to start looking for the real freedom of a fully informed choice.

CHAPTER 15

The Insensitivity Syndrome

We mentioned earlier that mankind is constantly seeking to refine its moral and ethical understanding. As with all other areas of society, this process could be influenced by false motives and ideas. I think it is important to consider how this can happen.

It has already been mentioned how the display of sex in magazines, advertising and movies has become more widespread. The same holds true for violence and killing. For anyone willing to compare the movies today with those of 30 or so years ago, it will be easy to notice a tremendous difference. There is more violence in today's movies, far more, and it is shown in a different light. In a growing number of popular movies, violence and killing (even mass killing) is glorified and presented as an acceptable way to resolve a conflict. Sometimes even as the better or at least the most efficient way of resolving conflict. Are we being conditioned to accept the use of force as the only means for resolving conflict?

It is easy to spot the growing fascination with death and the symbols and subjects relating to death. This can be seen in advertising, books, magazines, movies and, of course, on TV. A result of the fascination with violence, death and killing could very well be a growing insensitivity to life.

If we want to have the full perspective on the abortion debate, we might need to consider the psychological aspects behind insensitivity. In *People of the Lie*, Scott Peck describes two of the main characteristics of evil. The first one is the insensitivity to life, which Peck calls narcissism. The other is the extreme drive for evil to remain hidden, to avoid being recognized or recognized as evil. Peck describes an interesting mechanism. One of the psychologists seeking to describe evil was Erich Fromm, who based his theories on a study of Nazism and some of the Nazi leaders. As a result, his work has been looked upon as a study of the extreme, the exception. But as Peck points out, some of his patients may be no better than Nazi leaders; they simply have less opportunity to express their insensitivity on a large scale. Many supposedly normal citizens could be triggered into showing the same insensitivity. This can happen through the element of doubt, which is the open door for the lie to enter our consciousness.

Even for people who do not believe in the Bible as a factual account of creation, it is impossible to ignore that it can teach us many lessons about human psychology. How did the serpent persuade Eve to eat the forbidden fruit? When he first suggested it, she completely refused because she had a firm belief that she would die if she ate of the tree. What was the serpent's reply? "Ye shalt not surely die!" By that one word "surely" the element of doubt was induced and immediately Eve became "a house divided against itself." Although she may have reasoned back and forth for a while, the element of doubt finally caused her consciousness to shift to the opposite extreme.

This is what we could call "serpentine logic" and it is the hallmark of everyone who is seeking to manipulate other people. Call them necrophiliacs, people of the lie or the power elite, the word doesn't really matter as they are all expressing the same type of psychology.

This element of doubt can be used to neutralize inalienable rights. When people believe in the inalienable right to life, this is neutralized by introducing a new right that supposedly divides what before was conceived as undividable. Surely the right to life is a fundamental right, but so is the right to freedom of choice isn't it? Of course it is wrong to kill life and of course a fetus is human life, but a fetus is not a human person and therefore abortion is not surely killing—right?

Once doubt has opened the door, insensitivity will grow through a gradual process in which people become accustomed to the misuse of life. When it happens on a large enough scale, an entire population can become numbed, insensitive. They will suddenly begin to ignore a misuse of life that only a few years earlier would have caused them to be outraged. In other words, a society can be catapulted from one viewpoint into the opposite extreme, from reverence for life to complete insensitivity. There are several elements in this process:

1. *The introduction of doubt.* People's intuitive feeling for what is right and wrong must be neutralized. When people believe in a true idea, the way to neutralize it is to induce another idea that causes people to be divided within themselves. Maybe what we believe isn't really an absolute truth? Maybe we don't have the right to make other people follow what we believe is an absolute truth? Anyway, who am I to say what is right and wrong when all the big shots in society can't even tell?

2. *The gradual numbing of sensitivity.* As we have mentioned, the sexual revolution caused a numbing to the life creating process and its result; the child in the womb.

Violence, sex and symbols of death displayed everywhere in people's daily lives will gradually, especially for people who have been exposed to it from childhood, cause a numbing. People can only be outraged so many times, and then they begin to withdraw, especially when they see the so-called elite of their society promoting the images of death.

Another aspect of this principle is the numbing effect of numbers. When the child next door gets hurt, we can immediately relate to it and we react emotionally. But when 55 million babies are aborted each year, it assumes such enormous proportions that our emotions can no longer cope. The result is that we withdraw from the situation because we are not capable of producing an emotional reaction.

3. *The threat:* Yes, we all have to defend life and certainly an unborn baby is life. But if we don't limit the population growth, we will be setting the stage for disaster in the (near) future. What do you want, short-term sensitivity to life in the form of a few unborn babies, who are not even real persons, or long-term

sensitivity to the entire human race? What is the point in having babies born when all they can look forward to is poverty and starvation? Wouldn't it be better for them not to be born and better for the rest of us, too?

4. *The scapegoat.* According to Scott Peck, one of the characteristics of people of the lie is their tendency for scapegoating. This is really a tendency we all have and it is just one of the ways we can see the necrophilic tendencies in our psychology. A manipulator can play on this tendency by trying to make it look as if there is one group of people that is causing the problem, such as the unborn who are a threat to those already born. This also gives us an easy way out because it makes it seem as if it will only be the scapegoat that will be affected by the proposed solution to the problem. The rest of us can live happily ever after, and we don't have to change our lifestyle, much less our attitude.

Please take note that this discourse is not an attempt to say that everyone who is for abortion is a necrophiliac or is a supporter of evil. It is an attempt to point out how tendencies in our consciousness can be triggered by certain stimuli through the mechanics of mass-psychology.

Mass Psychology

History is full of bizarre examples of people reacting under the influence of mass psychology. This can especially be seen in crowds, and the first person to make a systematic study of the crowd and its psychology was the French scientist, Gustave LeBon. He based his studies on the reactions of crowds during the French revolution.

LeBon found that when people are assembled in a crowd, they lose their ability to reason, to go within, to discriminate. A crowd becomes a single entity acting with one mind. By controlling this mass mind, it is possible to control every person in the crowd. In a crowd, the individual sacrifices his personal interests for that of the crowd. He gives up his personal responsibility and begins to look to a central power for a solution to his problems. Since personal responsibility is one side of personal freedom, it follows that a crowd overpowers individual freedom.

LeBon found that the improbable does not exist for a crowd. In other words, a crowd tends to follow an "ends-justify-the-means" attitude and no means are unacceptable to a crowd. LeBon discovered how certain words or phrases have an extremely powerful effect on crowds. He said that reason cannot combat the effects of certain words or formulas on a crowd, and these words will cause everyone to obey instantly. During the French revolution, specific phrases were used repeatedly to arouse a crowd to kill. Indeed, the most out-standing effect of a crowd is that it can instantaneously turn a normal person into a killer. The crowd can convince people that killing is socially acceptable, that it is in the best overall in-terest of society. When people become influenced by such a mass psychology, their entire value and belief systems become momentarily altered.

What we have to consider is that today it is no longer necessary to assemble a crowd in the town square to create mass psychology. Modern technology has made it a lot easier and it is all said in the word itself—we call it mass media. Through mass media it is possible to exploit crowd psycholo-gy without ever physically assembling a crowd. All you have to do is get millions of people to sit down in front of their TV screens to watch the same channels day after day.

The Value Free Society

In his book *Generation of Narcissus*, Henry Malcolm says that today we are watching the creation of a new pheno-menon, the mass culture. This is not a real culture but a syn-thetic culture fabricated and induced by the mass media. The purpose is to promote a certain social system, to sell common goods and to spread the illusion of common values. The mass culture is a system of interlocking institutions acting as if there were no values except the survival and growth of the system itself. The result of the mass culture is a value free experimen-tal society. A society with no eternal values, based on an "any-thing goes" attitude, or rather, a society with only one absolute value: the system or the state.

Such a society is a lie since it is impossible to create a soci-ety with no values. Any society will automatically reflect the values of those controlling its institutions. Which brings us to the question of who controls the mass media. A handful of private corporations owns the major TV networks and thereby decide what people should see and hear about the world. A majority of the newspapers get most of their international news from only two wire services. In a democracy, everyone has a vote and everyone's vote counts the same. People can only vote based on what they know. If someone was seeking to control a democratic nation, what would be the first institution they would seek to gain control over?

Beginning in the 60s, the mass media launched a very intense campaign seeking to induce a sense of limitation in the general population. The idea is that this planet is a limited sphere and that life is defined by a set of limitations. Only so many people can survive on the planet, only so many resources are available and only so much wealth can be created. Therefore, the major, or only, problem facing mankind is too many people. According to LeBon, certain phrases will trigger an emotional reaction in the mind of the crowd. Does it seem far-fetched to say that expressions like "the population bomb" or "the population explosion" or "Famine '75" and "limits to growth" have triggered an emotional reaction in the minds of the people. Could this reaction have had an impact on the abortion debate?

The outcome of this media campaign is the widespread acceptance of the idea that we must all voluntarily accept certain limitations for how we can live and how our society can evolve. In the early '60s, most people marveled at the technological progress. They saw further technological adventures as the hope for bringing about a new and better age, and they realized it was technology that brought us out of the Dark Ages. They generally believed we could solve most of our material problems through technology. This optimism has been almost completely aborted and catapulted into the other extreme. Today most people believe technology has created most of our environmental problems and that it is dangerous. Therefore, the free enterprise use of technology must be controlled and restricted to prevent disaster.

Have we, meaning the general population, gradually been conditioned to accept the insensitivity to life and the sense of limitation that has always been the hallmark of power elites?

CHAPTER 16

The Question of Money

For some people the bottom line in the abortion debate is money and I think we should take a closer look at the economic aspects of abortion. There are three main elements.

Tax Burden

Some people claim that abortion relieves society of the immediate tax burden of a welfare baby, because most unwanted pregnancies occur in the poor part of the population. Therefore, society will have to take care of the babies.

Even if this was true, we still have to consider that it would not be a complete loss to society. One of the driving forces in the economy is that people have to consume certain goods to survive. The tax money spent on a welfare baby will all be recycled into the economy to buy food, clothing, housing, transportation, baby-sitting and so on.

In the current economic situation, many people believe that one of the ways to give the economy a boost is public spending. Expanding and improving the highways is proposed as one way to boost the economy and create new jobs. Well, spending tax money on keeping millions of welfare babies alive would most certainly create new jobs too. What is the real difference between spending tax money on highways and spending it on babies, when both ways will boost the economy and create jobs? One major difference is the difference between a lifeless concrete structure and a living, breathing person. But let us keep talking money. Surely the highways are an investment that will yield an economic return, but wouldn't the babies? Even a welfare baby will be a consumer and thereby keep the economy going. Welfare babies too can grow up to become solid, middle class citizens who are paying their taxes. Some of today's middle class people are children of relatively poor parents. They became middle class because being born in poverty gave them a drive to strive for a better position.

Another aspect is the possibility that some of these welfare babies could give a unique contribution to society, as we mentioned earlier. Many of the so-called great men and women of history were born and raised by poor parents.

Today's baby is tomorrow's taxpayer. If there are no babies, there eventually will be no taxpayers. Then who is going to pay the taxes when today's taxpayers have retired? We know today that in most western nations, the population is "aging" with the percentage of retired people increasing, while the percentage of people in their productive age is decreasing. When will we reach the critical point in which there are no longer enough people working to support the amount of retirees? Has 25 million abortions done anything to speed up this process?

In Third World countries, the mechanism is recognized by all. It is your children who will have to support you when you get too old to work, so you must have enough children to carry the burden. In our rich nations this is still true although it is done indirectly through taxes—no children, no taxes, no pensions.

The Value of a Person

The essence of this argumentation can be found in an article from 1966 written by Steven Enki entitled, "Economic Aspects of Slowing Population Growth" and published by *Economic Journal*. Enki set up some figures showing that the value of consumption expenditures of a new child was more than his total productivity in his active life. The child would consume more than he produced. Therefore, society would be economically better off without him.

First, the model used was not correct since it was developed by treating a person like a thing with a relative yearly discount rate on his value of 10 to 15%. This is a fairly high discount rate and as any student of economy will confirm, a future income can always be reduced to zero by setting the discount rate high enough.

The second problem with this argumentation is that it is not logical. Even if it is true that a person consumes more than he produces, then how can this be a detriment to the economy? The driving force in a free market economy is demand; if there is no demand there is no basis for economic growth. If people consume more than they produce, then demand will tend to be higher than supply, and that is the very foundation for economic growth. If the demand goes up, someone will start producing more to get a share of the profit.

What Enki was really saying was that by slowing down population growth, we can slow down economic growth. Before we had examined the power elite, this would not have made sense to us because we would have been unable to see any motive for slowing down economic growth. Now we realize that the power elite with their psychology of limitation is constantly seeking to stop all growth and create a stable, no-growth society in which they are in control. When you have a monopoly on wealth, you don't need economic growth. If you cannot stop it completely, you want to slow it down to a rate that allows you to stay in control.

Resources and Standard of Living

This argumentation states that the available resources divided by the number of people will determine the standard of living. If the amount of resources is fixed, it will inevitably lower the standard of living when more people have to share them. The only way to raise the standard of living is to lower the number of people. The basis for this argumentation must be the assumption that it is impossible to increase the amount of resources because the planet only has so many raw-materials.

As we have already examined, the amount of resources is not a fixed amount but can be expanded greatly. The way to do so is through individual creativity, by allowing an economy in which individual effort is rewarded justly. This will happen quite automatically as demand rises. This kind of economy is called free enterprise.

The argumentation, furthermore, assumes that all available resources are distributed evenly. History shows us that this is not a reality because there is always an elite with a drive to get more than a fair share of the resources. In reality, the argumentation completely ignores the perspective of the power elite.

The reason the general population has an undesirable standard of living may not be a lack of resources. We see from history, that in most cases, the real cause is a monopolization of wealth in the hands of an elite. Lowering the number of people on the planet is no guarantee that the standard of living will be increased. If the power elite is allowed to continue their monopoly, the standard of living will stay the same no matter how much the population decreases. What is guaranteed, however, is that a lower number of people will make it easier for the power elite to stay in control because it diminishes the need for social change.

In the recession today, one of the factors most often mentioned as the way to bring the economy back on track is consumer spending. This can only happen if there are consumers and if they have money to spend. If abortion had not been legalized in 1973, there would have been over 25 million more consumers in the United States today. Would we have had a recession if there had been that many more consumers? Have we, by aborting these 25 million potential consumers, aborted the means for either preventing or overcoming the recession? We do have a number of very sophisticated computer models for predicting economic developments. I think they should be put to use in answering the question of how our economic situation would have been today if the 25 million abortions had not been performed.

The Awful Truth About a Free Market Economy

In some of the previous chapters I have talked about a more equal or just distribution of wealth and I am aware that this will cause some people to label me as a socialist. So, I would like to make it clear, that I do not believe in Marxism, Communism or any form of Socialism and neither do I believe in

Capitalism. I know some people believe Capitalism and free enterprise are the same thing and I used to think so too, but let us take a closer look at this popular paradigm.

First, let us tackle one of the most subtle and widely believed lies about a free market economy, that a free economy creates and encourages greed and selfishness.

This is not true. A free economy is based on the principle that as you sow, so shall you reap. If you work harder or are more creative, you will give a higher service to life, then you will be entitled to a higher compensation from life. In a truly free economy, the person or company providing the best service to its customers will always get the best return. In reality, a free economy encourages selfless service or quality products because you don't get something for nothing. If you provide lousy service, people will buy from someone else.

As we learned previously, some people are not capable of rendering a selfless service. To a necrophiliac, selflessness is an impossible idea. Therefore, a necrophiliac will not do well in a system where he will be rewarded according to his service. He wants a system that makes it possible for him to reap without sowing. He wants something for nothing by creating a situation where people cannot buy from someone else.

What we have to realize is that selfishness and greed are not a product of a free market economy, they are the product of an ego-centered consciousness.

In the 1800's, there was a drive among big businessmen to form trusts to create monopolies. The idea was that if you have a monopoly on supply, you can demand any price you want. What most people are not aware of is that it is not possible to maintain a monopoly in a free market economy. If someone gains a monopoly on the supply of certain goods and raises the price, then it automatically raises the incentive for someone else to break the monopoly and get a share of the action. Breaking a monopoly is extremely easy as long as the economy is free. All it takes is someone who is willing to settle for a lower profit. If he starts manufacturing the same product and selling it for a lower price than the monopolists, the monopoly is already ended, because most people will want to save money and buy at the lowest price! Other ways to break a monopoly is to develop a similar product that works better, to come up with a more efficient manufacturing process, or to invent a new product, making the old one obsolete. The only way to maintain a monopoly is to neutralize people's inconvenient drive to buy at the lowest price. The only way to do that is to turn a free market economy into an organized economy with central control of prices. In a democratic nation this can only be done through the government, which is the only centralized power allowed by the Constitution.

This may indeed be what happened in the early 1900s. The powerful financiers and industrialists in the United States were convinced about one absolute truth. No great monetary wealth can ever be accumulated under the impartial rules of a free market economy. The only sure road to accumulation of massive wealth is a monopoly. Gaining a monopoly means killing free enterprise by turning it into an economic system with central control. In this way monopoly can be gained through government regulations!

Many people believe that in the late 1800s, the government, through the populist reforms, sought to end monopolies. What they don't know is that although the populists were seeking to reform big business, big business was working even harder to become reformed. The leading industrialists were fully aware that they were at a crossroads. Their drive to form monopolies was clearly illegal and would undermine the very democracy that had given them the freedom to organize these monopolies. The industrialists knew that they had only two options: They could either break with the existing political system, or they could reform the system so it would allow them to carry out their agenda. They could make it look as if monopolies were in the best interests of the public good, so they would be sanctioned by the government. Of course, we don't call it monopoly anymore. It is disguised as an attempt to protect society from the turbulence of a free economy by inducing an element of stability into the economy.

To protect "society" from the exploitation caused by the greed and selfishness that is allowed to develop in a free market economy, we must impose regulations. These regulations must restrict the element of competition which is portrayed as the core of the problem.

What is overlooked is that by restricting free competition, we make it harder for new businesses to challenge the position of established businesses. This solidifies the position of the old companies and automatically creates an elite with a privileged position.

By formulating the problem in the "right way," we can turn everything upside down. Greed and selfishness are portrayed as the inevitable result of a free market economy in which anyone can launch a new enterprise any way he wants. In reality, greed and selfishness are the hallmarks of the power elite, and they cannot thrive in a free economy if the people are enlightened. Free competition is portrayed as the very thing that leads to the formation of monopolies. In reality, free competition will inevitably overturn monopolies as quickly as they can be formed.

I earlier described how an attempt to prevent the use of false ideas will take away the very freedom that a democracy is meant to give. The same holds true for a free market economy. If a government seeks to prevent the misuse of market forces, it will remove free competition and thereby the government itself becomes an instrument for the destruction of the free economy. Capitalism is an economic system and as all systems it can be controlled by a central authority. Free enterprise is not a system and thus it cannot be controlled by a small elite and that is why the elite wants to get away from it. Free enterprise does not give everyone the same amount of wealth, it gives an equal economic opportunity to all so that a person's wealth is determined by his or her own, principle-centered efforts. This will lead to a just distribution of wealth, as long as the people are alert and informed. I believe the only viable alternative to government control is an enlightened media combined with a number of consumer protection and information groups. The reason being that in a democracy knowledge is the ultimate form of power.

In a totalitarian society, you can dominate others through force, in a democracy you can only dominate others if they allow you to do so by their freewill choice. Since people would not allow themselves to be manipulated if they knew better, it follows that the key-factor is knowledge. The more people know, the less they can be manipulated by anyone.

I believe the main purpose of life is to grow in understanding and that is why I think a democracy with a true free market economy is the ideal society. In a democracy there is no excuse for ignorance. When we have complete freedom, it is our own responsibility to educate ourselves to the point that no one can take advantage of us. We cannot allow anyone, not even the government, to be responsible for our education about the deeper aspects of life, because then we are giving away our freedom. A democracy is actually a very tough society because it places all responsibility and accountability upon the individual citizen. If we are not sufficiently informed, we really cannot blame anyone but ourselves because the information is out there somewhere. It was our choice not to put in a greater effort to find that information. Eternal vigilance is the price we must pay for democracy.

Let me conclude by saying that even though I have tried to gather a great deal of information in this book, I by no means consider it to be the final word on abortion. Over the past decade I have systematically tried to free myself from all false ideas and motives, but I cannot know if this process is complete. The book can only be an expression of the level to which my understanding has progressed, so I hope you will seek additional information instead of taking my word for it. I think anyone, who would read the many books I have recommended would get a solid foundation for understanding what is going on in our world. I think this information would be a very efficient defense against manipulation and it would also open up for a new and much more exciting approach to life. I really think there is more to life than we were brought up to believe.

BIBLIOGRAPHY

Psychology and Self-help

Covey, Stephen R.*The 7 Habits of Highly Effective People.* New York: Simon & Schuster, 1989.

Fromm, Erich. *Escape From Freedom.* Avon, 1976.

Scott Peck, M. *People of the Lie: The Hope for Healing Human Evil.* New York: Simon & Schuster, 1983.

— *The Road Less Traveled.* New York: Simon & Schuster.

Religion/Christianity

Booth, Father Leo. *When God Becomes a Drug.* J. P. Tarche, 1991.

Brown, Schuyler. *The Origins of Christianity: A Historical Introduction to the New Testament.* Oxford and New York: Oxford University Press, 1984.

Howe, Quincy. *Reincarnation for the Christian.* Theosophical Publishing House, 1987.

Pagels, Elaine M. *The Gnostic Gospels.* New York: Random House, 1979.

— *The Gnostic Paul. Gnostic Exegesis of the Pauline Letters.* Philadelphia: Fortress Press. 1975.

Prophet, Elizabeth Clare. *The Lost Years of Jesus.* Los Angeles: Summit University Press, 1984.

Robinson, James M. *The Nag Hammadhi Library in English.* New York: Harper & Row, 1977.

Smith, Morton. *The Secret Gospel: The Discovery and Interpretation of the Secret Gospel According to Mark.* New York: Harper & Row, 1973.

Near-death Experiences

Eadie, Betty J. *Embraced by the Light.* Gold Leaf Print, 1992.

Wambach, Helen. *Life Before Life.* New York: Bantam, 1984

Whitton, Dr. Joel L. and Fischer, Joe. *Life Between Life.* Warner Books, 1988.

The New Science
Augros, Robert and Stanciu, George. *The New Story of Science*. New York: Bantam, 1986.
Capra, Fridtjof. *The Tao of Physics*. Berkeley. Calif: Shambhala , 1975
Davies, Paul. *The Mind of God*. New York: Simon & Schuster, 1992.
Herbert, Nick. *Quantum Reality*. New York: Doubleday, 1985
Pagels, Heinz R., *The Cosmic Code*. New York: Simon & Schuster, 1980.
Peat, David. *Synchronicity*. New York: Bantam, 1987.
Zukav, Gary. *The Dancing Wu Li Masters*. New York: Morrow, 1979.

Democracy and History
Chase, Alston. *Playing God in Yellowstone*. New York: Harcourt Brace Jovanovich, 1986
Domhoff, William G. *Who Rules America Now?* New York: Simon & Schuster, 1986.
Dye, Thomas R. and Zeigler, Harmon. *The Irony of Democracy,* Wadsworth Publishing, 1993.
Huxley, Aldous. *Brave New World.* Buccaneer Books, 1982.
Malcolm, Henry. *Generation of Narcissus.*
Orwell, George. *1984.* New York: Harcourt Brace Jovanovich, 1949.
Revel, Jean-Francois. *How Democracies Perish*. New York: Harper & Row, 1983.
Skousen, Willard Cleon. *The Naked Capitalist*. New York: Author, 1970.
Sutton Antony C. *An Introduction to the Order.* Res Pubns, 1983.
— *How the Order Creates War and Revolution.* Res Pubns, 1984.
— *How the Order Controls Education.* Res Pubns, 1983

INDEX

Emotional energy, 28, 30, 34.
Emotional pain, 11, 14, 33, 80.
Emotional self-defense, 21.
Ends-justify-the-means, 18, 151, 175.
Enki, Steven, 178.
Enlightened self-interest, 19, 23, 28, 32, 69, 88.
Environment. problems, 127, 147.
Erlich, Paul, 141
Ethics, 26, 62.
Ethnic conflict, 10, 99.
Eugenics, 139.
Evil, 27, 74, 172.
Evolution, 37, 138

Faith, 38, 47.
False ideas, 32, 42, 58, 123, 158.
False motives, 32, 42, 58.
Fatalism, 138.
Fetus, 80, 85, 119, 172.
Feudal society, 17, 129, 132.
Fifth Ecumenical Council, 42, 45.
Fischer, Joe, 64.
Forbidden Question, 13.
Freedom, 18, 22, 33, 44, 67, 91, 104, 147, 155.
Freedom of choice, 157.
Free market economy, 179.
Free will, 50, 67, 74, 94, 113, 157
Free will, misuse of, 67, 74.
Fromm, Eric, 122, 145, 172.
Fundamental Questions, 38, 44, 54, 58, 64, 71.

Galton, Francis, 134.
Gnosticism, 41.
God, 50, 66, 71, 81, 91, 138.
God's will, 68.
Golden Rule, 68, 135, 143.
Good and evil, 25.
Gordian Knot, 31, 148.
Government, 24, 111, 159, 182.

Grace period, 107.
Gravity, 24, 50.
Grass-root effort, 161.
Greed, 181.
Growth, 11, 33, 64, 76, 98, 160.
Guilt, 73, 83, 90, 128, 165.

Happiness, 23, 28, 65, 104.
Heaven, 61.
Hell, 61.
Herbert, Nick, 54.
Heredity, 138.
Hippocrates, 141.
Hitler, Adolf, 74, 134, 140.
Howe, Quincy, 64.
Human nature, 19, 23
Human rights, 77
Humanism, 32.
Hypnotic regression, 64, 78.

Incest, 78.
Inalien. rights, 26, 119, 156, 172.
Industrial revolution, 132.
Infertility, 103.
Informed choice, 105, 159, 170.
Injustice, 17.
Insensitivity, 171.
Intellect, 25, 27, 32
Intuition, 26, 97.

Jesus, 40, 46, 88, 152.
Judeo-Christian tradition, 39.
Jung, Carl, 26, 29.
Just cause, 21.
Justice, 22, 73.

Killing, 171
Kuhn, Thomas, 11.

Laws of nature, 67, 73, 81, 89.
Laws of physics, 51.
Laws of society, 20, 31, 77.
Law of the jungle, 17, 62, 120.

Order Form

Ordering by Phone: Call 406-333-4513
Ordering by Mail: Fill out this form and mail it to: **More to Life Publishing**
P.O. Box 92, Emigrant, MT 59027, USA

Please send me the following books.

_____ Forbidden Questions About Abortion. $ 12.95 per book

_____ What They Don't Want You to Know About Anti-hunting. $ 8.00 per book

Ship books to: _____

_____ State_____ Zip_____ Phone_____

Shipping: **FREE.**
Please make checks or money orders payable to More to Life Publishing